# Betty Crocker's
# PASTA
# Favorites

PRENTICE HALL

New York    London    Toronto    Sydney    Tokyo    Singapore

PRENTICE HALL GENERAL REFERENCE
15 Columbus Circle
New York, New York, 10023

**Library of Congress Cataloging-in-Publication data**

Crocker, Betty
    Betty Crocker's pasta favorites.
        p.    cm.
    Includes index.
    ISBN 0-671-86516-1
    1. Cookery (Pasta) I. Title. II. Title: Pasta favorites.
TX809.M17C76   1993
641.8′22—dc20                    92-34872
                                 CIP


Designed by Levavi & Levavi
Manufactured in the United States of America

10  9  8  7  6  5  4  3  2  1

First Edition

Front Cover: Vermicelli with Fresh Herbs (page 18)
Back Cover: Pasta Shells with Chicken and Broccoli (page 36)

# Contents

**Introduction**                                    v

**Cooking Pasta Perfectly**                         vi

**1   Homemade Pasta, Homemade Sauces**    1

**2   Meatless Pasta**                             17

**3   Poultry and Pasta**                          33

**4   Seafood and Pasta**                          47

**5   Meat and Pasta**                             61

**Index**                                          81

# Introduction

=====■=====

Pasta seems to become more popular with every passing day, and it's no wonder when you consider that it's perfect as a main dish for dinner or lunch, or to serve as a side dish. It's also a boon to busy cooks because many pasta dishes are quick to prepare, as well as tasty and nutritious.

BETTY CROCKER'S PASTA FAVORITES presents pasta in its many delicious forms. Beginning with a chapter on homemade pasta and homemade sauces, you can have the pleasure of creating your own pasta and sauces, from basic Egg Noodles and classic Italian tomato sauce, to Pumpkin Ravioli and a sophisticated Mushroom and Brandy Sauce.

Next you'll find meatless pasta, with recipes for main dishes, salads and side dishes. You'll find comforting Macaroni and Cheese, hearty Cheesy Lasagne and refreshing Mostaccioli with Bell Pepper and Basil, as well as many other satisfying dishes. This chapter is particularly useful when you're looking for a dish to accompany a main course, or when you'd like a light pasta dish.

The following chapters collect recipes for pasta with poultry, seafood and meat. All you need to do is pick the category that suits your mood, and you'll find wonderful recipes. Sample Linguine with Chicken and Artichoke Hearts, Turkey Tortellini Soup, Baja Chicken-Pasta Salad, Angel Hair Pasta with Shrimp, Dilled Pasta Salad with Smoked Shrimp, Manicotti or Spaghetti and Meatballs, and make dinner special.

We have included everything you'll need to know to turn you into a pasta pro. From how to cook pasta perfectly, with cooking timetables, to how to identify the many forms of pasta, you'll find tips and suggestions that make BETTY CROCKER'S PASTA FAVORITES a book that will no doubt become one of your favorites.

*THE BETTY CROCKER EDITORS*

# Cooking Pasta Perfectly

Cooking pasta is quite simple when you follow the techniques below.

- Today people have discovered that they like their pasta as the Italians prefer it, *al dente* (literally "to the tooth," meaning tender but firm). Because mushy pasta loses much of its flavor and character, taste pasta before the recommended cooking time is up. That way, you can stop cooking it just when it reaches the stage you like best.

- Some cooks advise adding oil to the cooking water to keep pasta from sticking—to itself and to the pot. When pasta sticks, it's usually because the water stopped boiling when the pasta was added. It isn't necessary to add oil. Just be sure that the water is at a rapid, rolling boil when you add the pasta, that when you add it, the water doesn't stop boiling, and that you have used enough water.

- How much water should you use? About 3 quarts of water are needed for every 8 ounces of pasta. When the water comes to a boil, add a good pinch of salt if you like; let the water return to a rolling boil before adding pasta.

- Some dried pasta shapes are too large to be submerged all at once. Place one end of lasagne, spaghetti or other long pasta in the water; as it softens, gently push it down into the water.

- Draining noodles is an important step in preparing pasta dishes as it instantly stops the cooking. Draining should be done quickly, to prevent noodles from sticking together or cooling down. If the recipe calls for it, you can add some Parmesan cheese while mixing the noodles and sauce, to help sauce cling to the noodles. Don't add oil or rinse noodles in cold water (unless you are making a pasta salad), as it cools the noodles and makes them too slippery to receive a sauce.

How much pasta do you need to cook? Just follow this handy guide for serving amounts.

## PASTA YIELDS

| UNCOOKED PASTA | COOKED CUPS | PASTA SERVINGS |
| --- | --- | --- |
| Macaroni 6–7 ounces (2 cups) | 4 | 4–6 |
| Spaghetti 7–8 ounces | 4 | 4–6 |
| Noodles 8 ounces | 4–5 | 4–6 |
| Homemade pasta 12–14 ounces | 4 | 4–6 |

This timetable will tell you how long to cook your pasta. Test slightly before minimum cooking time to avoid overcooking.

## PASTA COOKING TIMETABLE

| FRESH HOMEMADE PASTA | COOKING TIME |
| --- | --- |
| Fettuccine | 5 to 7 minutes |
| Lasagne | 15 to 20 minutes |
| Noodles | 5 to 7 minutes |
| Ravioli | 12 to 14 minutes |
| Tortellini | 25 to 30 minutes |

Cook dried homemade pasta a few minutes longer than fresh.

| DRIED PACKAGED PASTA | COOKING TIME |
| --- | --- |
| Alphabets | 4 to 5 minutes |
| Anelli | 9 to 10 minutes |
| Ditalini | 8 to 9 minutes |
| Elbow Macaroni | 8 to 10 minutes |
| Farfalle | 11 to 12 minutes |
| Fettuccine | 10 to 12 minutes |
| Lasagne | 10 to 12 minutes |
| Linguine | 8 to 10 minutes |
| Manicotti | 10 to 12 minutes |
| Mostaccioli | 12 to 14 minutes |
| Noodles | 6 to 8 minutes |
| Orzo or Rosmarina | 5 to 8 minutes |
| Rigatoni | 14 to 16 minutes |
| Rotini | 10 to 12 minutes |
| Shell Macaroni   Small | 6 to 8 minutes |
| Medium | 10 to 12 minutes |
| Jumbo | 12 to 15 minutes |
| Spaghetti | 8 to 10 minutes |
| Tortellini | 25 to 30 minutes |
| Vermicelli | 4 to 6 minutes |
| Ziti | 12 to 14 minutes |

## PASTA IDENTIFICATION GUIDE

The many varieties of pasta on the market offer a fascinating assortment of sizes and shapes. This guide will help you to understand the various shapes and sizes.

## PASTA DESCRIPTION AND USE

| SPECIFIC NAME | SHAPE | DESCRIPTION | USE |
|---|---|---|---|
| **MACARONI** | | | |
| Alphabets | | tiny pasta alphabet | soups |
| Anelli | | tiny pasta rings | soups |
| Conchiglie | | smooth or ridged shell-shaped pasta in several sizes | soups or stuffed |
| Ditali | | large pasta "thimbles" with ridges | casseroles, salads, soups or with sauces |
| Elbow macaroni | | curved tubes in a variety of sizes and lengths | casseroles, soups |
| Farfalle | | pasta shaped like bows in a variety of sizes and colors | soups, stuffings |
| Lumache | | small- to medium-size snail-shaped pasta | casseroles, salads or with sauces |
| Macaroni | | pasta tubes in a variety of sizes and shapes | casseroles or soups |
| Mostaccioli | | medium-size pasta tubes with diagonally cut ends | served with hearty meat or tomato sauce |
| Orzo | | tiny pasta resembling oats | soups or cooked like rice |
| Rigatoni | | slightly curved small tubes | casseroles or soups |
| Risini | | tiny rice-shaped pasta | soups |
| Ziti | | short, smooth tubes | casseroles |
| **NOODLES** | | | |
| Fettuccine | | about ¼-inch-wide ribbon noodles, straight or in coils | buttered or in rich meat sauce |
| Lasagne | | wide pasta, sometimes with curly edges | baked dishes |

| SPECIFIC NAME | SHAPE | DESCRIPTION | USE |
|---|---|---|---|
| Noodle flakes | | very fine egg pasta sheets cut into ¼-inch squares | soups |
| Tagliatelle | | ¾-inch-wide egg noodles | casseroles or with sauces |
| **SPAGHETTI** | | | |
| Bucatini | | typical spaghetti but hollow instead of solid | with sauces |
| Capellini | | thin, often coiled, spaghetti | with sauces |
| Fusilli | | strands of spiral-shaped pasta | with sauces |
| Linguine | | flat, narrow, long | casseroles or with sauces |
| Spaghettini | | long, fine-cut strands of spaghetti | with sauces |
| Vermicelli | | straight or folded strands of very thin spaghetti | with sauces |
| **MISCELLANEOUS PASTA** | | | |
| Cannelloni | | 4- to 6-inch pieces of large, fresh pasta rolled around a filling | baked with sauces |
| Manicotti | | large smooth or ridged pasta tubes | cooked, filled with cheese or meat and baked |
| Ravioli | | pasta dumpling filled with spinach and ricotta cheese or meat and herbs | served with sauce |
| **OTHER** | | | |
| Cellophane noodles | | hard, clear white noodles made from mung beans; turn translucent when cooked in liquid, puffy and crisp when deep-fat fried | Oriental-style dishes |

## HOW TO USE NUTRITION INFORMATION

Nutrition Information per serving for each recipe includes the amounts of calories, protein, carbohydrate, fat, cholesterol and sodium.

- If ingredient choices are given, the first listed ingredient is used in recipe nutrition information calculations.

- When ingredient ranges or more than one serving size is indicated, the first weight or serving is used to calculate nutrition information.

- "If desired" ingredients and recipe variations are not included in nutrition information calculations.

# Menus

## QUICK WORKDAY DINNER

Pasta Shells with Chicken and Broccoli (page 36)
Sliced Cucumbers with Italian Dressing
Bread Sticks
Cookies and Grapes
Tea or Coffee

## HOT-WEATHER PASTA

Seafood-Pasta Salad (page 58)
Sliced Tomatoes and Onions
Pita Bread
Sherbet or Sorbet
Iced Tea

## HOMEMADE PASTA FOR DINNER

Tortelli with Olive Sauce (page 5)
Zucchini with Basil
Spumoni Ice Cream and Amaretti Cookies
Wine or Fruit Juice

## COZY WINTER DINNER

Lasagne (page 62)
Tossed Green Salad
Garlic Bread
Apple Crisp
Milk

## PASTA FOR LUNCH

Tortellini and Sausage Soup (page 78)
Rolls and Butter
Milk

## COMPANY DINNER

Scallops in Cream Sauce (page 49)
Steamed Asparagus
Caesar Salad
Popovers
Strawberry Tart
Tea or Coffee

*Pumpkin Ravioli (page 9)*

# 1

# Homemade Pasta, Homemade Sauces

## Half-Shell Noodles with Broccoli and Ricotta Sauce

Egg Noodles (page 2)
2 tablespoons olive oil
2 cloves garlic, finely chopped
1 medium onion, chopped (about ½ cup)
3 cups broccoli flowerets
1 cup whole milk
½ cup chicken broth
4 quarts water
1 tablespoon salt
16 ounces ricotta cheese
½ cup grated Parmesan cheese
Freshly ground pepper

Prepare dough for Egg Noodles as directed; do not roll or cut. Divide dough into 12 equal parts. Roll each part into a rope, ½ inch thick. Cut each rope into ½-inch pieces. Place cut sides down on lightly floured surface. Press thumb in center of each piece, forming half-shells. Place on lightly floured towels.

Heat oil in 10-inch skillet over medium-high heat. Sauté garlic and onion in oil. Stir in broccoli, milk

and chicken broth. Heat to boiling; reduce heat. Cover and simmer about 10 minutes or until broccoli is tender.

Heat water and salt to boiling in large kettle; add noodles. Boil uncovered about 10 minutes, stirring occasionally, until *al dente* (tender but firm). Begin testing for doneness when noodles rise to surface of water. Drain noodles. Do not rinse. Mix broccoli mixture and ricotta and Parmesan cheeses; stir in noodles. Serve with pepper. **6 servings**

PER SERVING: Calories 370; Protein 20 g; Carbohydrate 34 g; Fat 17 g; Cholesterol 125 mg; Sodium 1450 mg

*Place a piece of dough on surface, cut side down. Press thumb in center, rotating thumb slightly to form a round indentation.*

# Egg Noodles

*Making your own pasta can be very satisfying, and well worth the time you spend.*

**3 cups semolina or all-purpose flour**
**4 jumbo eggs**
**¼ teaspoon salt**
**1 teaspoon olive oil**

Place flour in a mound on surface or in large bowl. Make a well in center of flour; add remaining ingredients. Mix thoroughly with fork, gradually bringing flour to center, until dough forms. (If dough is too sticky, gradually add flour when kneading. If dough is too dry, mix in enough water to make dough easy to handle.) Knead on lightly floured surface about 15 minutes or until smooth and elastic. Cover with plastic wrap or aluminum foil. Let stand 15 minutes.

Divide dough into 4 equal parts. (If desired, wrap unrolled dough securely and refrigerate up to 2 days. Let stand uncovered at room temperature 30 minutes before rolling and cutting.) Roll and cut as directed below.          **12 servings**

PER SERVING: Calories 145; Protein 6 g; Carbohydrate 24 g; Fat 3 g; Cholesterol 90 mg; Sodium 70 mg

MANUAL PASTA MACHINE: Flatten one part dough with hands to ½-inch thickness on lightly floured surface (keep remaining dough covered). Feed 1 part dough through smooth rollers set at widest setting. Sprinkle with all-purpose flour if dough becomes sticky. Fold lengthwise into thirds. Repeat feeding dough through rollers and folding into thirds 8 to 10 times or until firm and smooth. Feed dough through progressively narrower settings until dough is ⅛ to 1/16 inch thick. (Dough will lengthen as it becomes thinner; it may be cut crosswise at any time for easier handling.) Sprinkle dough lightly with all-purpose flour. Cut into ¼-inch strips for fettuccine, ⅛-inch strips for linguine.

HAND ROLLING: Roll each part dough with rolling pin into rectangle ⅛ to 1/16 inch thick on lightly floured surface. Sprinkle dough lightly with all-purpose flour. Loosely fold rectangle lengthwise into thirds; cut crosswise into ¼-inch strips for fettuccine, ⅛-inch strips for linguine. Shake out strips.

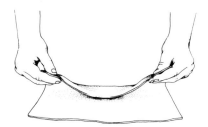

*Fold one-third of dough lengthwise slightly over center.*

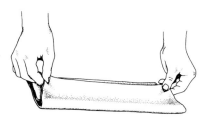

*Bring remaining side over folded dough.*

*Cut crosswise into ¼-inch strips for fettuccine or ⅛-inch strips for linguine.*

*al dente* (tender but firm). Begin testing for doneness when noodles rise to surface of water. Drain noodles. Do not rinse.

*\*If desired, let noodles stand at room temperature until completely dry. (Do not store until completely dry.) Dried noodles are very fragile; handle carefully. Cover loosely and store at room temperature up to 1 month.*

HALF-RECIPE EGG NOODLES: Cut all ingredients in half. Continue as directed.

Arrange noodles in single layer on lightly floured towels; sprinkle lightly with all-purpose flour. (Or hang noodles on rack.) Let stand uncovered at room temperature 30 minutes.* Cook immediately as directed below, or cover and refrigerate up to 2 days, arranged in single layer on lightly floured towels.

Heat 4 quarts water and 1 tablespoon salt to boiling in large kettle; add noodles. Boil uncovered 2 to 4 minutes, stirring occasionally, until

# Flour for Pasta

Semolina flour is made from durum wheat, a hard wheat high in protein. When ground it is yellow and has a coarse consistency similar to granulated sugar. Semolina is an excellent choice when making pasta, as it gives structure and elasticity to the pasta dough. All-purpose flour also produces excellent pasta. The dough is less stiff than dough made with semolina flour, and easier to handle. If you are making pasta for the first time, you may want to use all-purpose flour.

**Tortelli with Olive Sauce**

## Tortelli with Olive Sauce

*Try the caviar variation for special occasions.*

**Egg Noodles (page 2)**
**1 cup chopped fresh spinach**
**1 cup ricotta cheese, well drained**
**1 teaspoon grated Romano cheese**
**1 teaspoon grated nutmeg**
**2 tablespoons margarine or butter**
**1 small onion, thinly sliced**
**1 red bell pepper, finely chopped**
**¼ cup light rum, if desired**
**2 cups whipping (heavy) cream**
**¼ teaspoon grated nutmeg**
**¼ teaspoon salt**
**¼ teaspoon pepper**
**¼ cup black or green chopped olives, or**
**    1 jar (4 ounces) black or red caviar,**
**    drained**
**4 quarts water**
**1 tablespoon salt**
**¼ cup grated Parmesan cheese**

Prepare dough for Egg Noodles as directed; roll and cut into 14 rectangles, 12 × 4 inches. Cover rectangles with plastic wrap until ready to use.

Mix spinach, ricotta and Romano cheeses and 1 teaspoon nutmeg. Place ten 1-teaspoon mounds cheese mixture about 1½ inches apart in 2 rows on 1 rectangle. Moisten dough lightly around mounds with water; top with second rectangle. Press gently around mounds to seal.

Cut around mounds using 2-inch tortelli cutter or round cookie cutter. Arrange in single layer on lightly floured towels; sprinkle lightly with all-purpose flour. Repeat with remaining cheese mixture and rectangles. Let stand uncovered at room temperature 30 minutes. Cook tortelli immediately as directed below, or cover and refrigerate up to 2 days arranged in single layer on lightly floured towels.

Heat margarine in 10-inch skillet over medium-high heat. Sauté onion and bell pepper in margarine. Stir in rum if desired; cook until liquid is evaporated. Stir in whipping cream, ¼ teaspoon nutmeg, ¼ teaspoon salt and the pepper. Heat to boiling; reduce heat. Simmer uncovered 30 minutes, stirring frequently. Stir in olives. Cook 10 minutes longer, stirring frequently.

Heat water and 1 tablespoon salt to boiling in large kettle; add tortelli. Boil uncovered about 6 minutes, stirring occasionally, until *al dente* (tender but firm). Begin testing for doneness when tortelli rise to surface of water. Drain tortelli. Do not rinse. Pour sauce over tortelli; sprinkle with Parmesan cheese.

**6 servings**

PER SERVING: Calories 555; Protein 14 g; Carbohydrate 32 g; Fat 41 mg; Cholesterol 225 mg; Sodium 1460 mg

# Spinach Noodles

*A delicious variation on basic pasta.*

**1 package (10 ounces) frozen chopped spinach**
**3 cups semolina or all-purpose flour**
**3 eggs**
**¼ teaspoon salt**

Cook spinach as directed on package; squeeze or press out liquid. Finely chop spinach, or place in food processor or in blender; cover and process until smooth.

Place flour in a mound on surface or in large bowl. Make a well in center of flour; add spinach, eggs and salt. Mix thoroughly with fork, gradually bringing flour to center, until dough forms. (If dough is too sticky, gradually add flour when kneading. If dough is too dry, mix in water.) Knead on lightly floured surface about 15 minutes or until smooth and elastic. Cover with plastic wrap or aluminum foil. Let stand 15 minutes.

Divide dough into 4 equal parts. (If desired, wrap unrolled dough securely and refrigerate up to 2 days. Let stand at room temperature 30 minutes before rolling and cutting.) Roll and cut as directed below. **12 servings**

PER SERVING: Calories 140; Protein 5 g; Carbohydrate 25 g; Fat 2 g; Cholesterol 55 mg; Sodium 75 mg

MANUAL PASTA MACHINE: Flatten one part dough with hands to ½-inch thickness on lightly floured surface (keep remaining dough covered). Feed one part dough through smooth rollers set at widest setting. Sprinkle with all-purpose flour if dough becomes sticky. Fold lengthwise into thirds. Repeat feeding dough through rollers and folding into thirds 8 to 10 times or until firm and smooth. Feed dough through progressively narrower settings until dough is ⅛ to ¹⁄₁₆ inch thick. (Dough will lengthen as it becomes thinner; it may be cut crosswise at any time for easier handling.) Sprinkle dough lightly with all-purpose flour. Cut into ¼-inch strips for fettuccine, ⅛-inch strips for linguine.

HAND ROLLING: Roll each part dough with rolling pin into rectangle ⅛ to ¹⁄₁₆ inch thick on lightly floured surface. Sprinkle dough lightly with all-purpose flour. Loosely fold rectangle lengthwise into thirds; cut crosswise into ¼-inch strips for fettuccine, ⅛-inch strips for linguine. Shake out strips.

Arrange noodles in single layer on lightly floured towels; sprinkle lightly with all-purpose flour. (Or hang noodles on rack.) Let stand uncovered at room temperature 30 minutes.* Cook immediately as directed below, or cover and refrigerate up to 2 days, arranged in single layer on lightly floured towels.

Heat 4 quarts water and 1 tablespoon salt to boiling in large kettle; add noodles. Boil uncovered 2 to 4 minutes, stirring occasionally, until *al dente* (tender but firm). Begin testing for doneness when noodles rise to surface of water. Drain noodles. Do not rinse.

*If desired, let noodles stand at room temperature until completely dry. (Do not store until completely dry.) Dried noodles are very fragile; handle carefully. Cover loosely and store at room temperature up to 1 month.*

## Antonio's Fettuccine Alfredo

Egg Noodles (page 2)*
2 tablespoons butter
1 small onion, thinly sliced
4 cups whipping (heavy) cream
2 tablespoons freshly grated Parmesan
   cheese
1 teaspoon freshly grated nutmeg
½ teaspoon salt
½ teaspoon pepper
4 quarts water
1 tablespoon salt
2 tablespoons freshly grated Parmesan
   cheese
1 teaspoon freshly grated nutmeg
Freshly ground pepper

Prepare dough for Egg Noodles; roll and cut into fettuccine as directed. Remove one-third of the fettuccine and store for another use.

Heat butter in 10-inch skillet over medium-high heat. Sauté onion in butter. Stir in whipping cream; heat to boiling. Stir in 2 tablespoons cheese, 1 teaspoon nutmeg, ½ teaspoon salt and ½ teaspoon pepper; reduce heat. Simmer uncovered 30 minutes, stirring frequently.

Heat water and 1 tablespoon salt to boiling in large kettle; add fettuccine. Boil uncovered 2 to 4 minutes, stirring occasionally, until *al dente* (tender but firm). Begin testing for doneness when fettuccine rise to surface of water. Drain fettuccine. Do not rinse. Mix fettuccine and sauce; top with 2 tablespoons cheese and 1 teaspoon nutmeg. Serve with pepper.

**6 servings**

PER SERVING: Calories 690; Protein 11 g; Carbohydrate 30 g; Fat 58 g; Cholesterol 275 mg; Sodium 600 mg

*1 package (16 ounces) fresh or dried fettuccine can be substituted for the Egg Noodles. Cook as directed on package.*

## Straw and Hay Pasta

Egg Noodles (page 2)*
Spinach Noodles (page 6)**
2 tablespoons butter
2 tablespoons chopped fresh parsley
½ small onion, chopped (about 2
   tablespoons)
1½ cups sliced fresh mushrooms (about
   4 ounces)
4 ounces fully cooked smoked ham, cut
   into 1 × ¼-inch strips
¼ cup brandy
1 cup whipping (heavy) cream
¼ teaspoon salt
¼ teaspoon pepper
4 quarts water
1 tablespoon salt
1 cup freshly grated Parmesan cheese
Freshly ground pepper

Prepare dough for Egg Noodles and Spinach Noodles; roll and cut each into fettuccine as directed. Remove two-thirds of each fettuccine and store for another use.

Heat butter in 10-inch skillet over medium-high heat. Sauté parsley and onion in butter. Stir in mushrooms and ham. Cook about 5 minutes, stirring occasionally, until mushrooms are tender. Stir in brandy. Cook uncovered until liquid is evaporated. Stir in whipping cream, ¼ teaspoon salt and ¼ teaspoon pepper. Heat to boiling; reduce heat. Simmer uncovered about 15 minutes, stirring frequently, until thickened.

Heat water and 1 tablespoon salt to boiling in large kettle; add fettuccine. Boil uncovered 2 to 4 minutes, stirring occasionally, until *al dente* (tender but firm). Begin testing for doneness when fettuccine rise to surface of water. Drain fettuccine. Do not rinse. Mix fettuccine and sauce; top with cheese. Serve with pepper. **6 servings**

PER SERVING: Calories 415; Protein 18 g; Carbohydrate 29 g; Fat 25 g; Cholesterol 150 mg; Sodium 970 mg

*8 ounces fresh or dried fettuccine can be substituted for the Egg Noodles. Cook as directed on package.*
**8 ounces fresh or dried spinach fettuccine can be substituted for the Spinach Noodles. Cook as directed on package.*

## Ravioli with Bolognese Sauce

**Egg Noodles (page 2) or Spinach Noodles (page 6)**
**Bolognese Sauce (page 11)**
**1 cup chopped fresh spinach**
**16 ounces ricotta cheese**
**½ teaspoon grated nutmeg**
**¼ teaspoon salt**
**4 quarts water**
**1 tablespoon salt**
**Grated Parmesan cheese**

Prepare dough for Egg Noodles as directed; roll and cut into 14 rectangles, 12 × 4 inches. Cover rectangles with plastic wrap until ready to use. Prepare Bolognese Sauce; keep warm.

Mix spinach, ricotta cheese, nutmeg and ¼ teaspoon salt. Place ten 1-teaspoon mounds of cheese mixture about 1½ inches apart in 2 rows on 1 rectangle. Moisten dough lightly around mounds with water; top with second rectangle. Press gently around mounds to seal.

*Cut around mounds with 2-inch round cutter.*

Cut between mounds into 10 squares using pastry cutter of knife. Arrange in single layer on lightly floured towels; sprinkle lightly with all-purpose flour. Repeat with remaining cheese mixture and rectangles. Let stand uncovered at room temperature 30 minutes. Cook ravioli immediately as directed below, or cover and refrigerate up to 2 days arranged in single layer on lightly floured towels.

Heat water and 1 tablespoon salt to boiling in large kettle; add ravioli. Boil uncovered about 6 minutes, stirring occasionally, until *al dente* (tender but firm). Begin testing for doneness when ravioli rise to surface of water. Drain ravioli. Do not rinse. Top ravioli with sauce and sprinkle generously with Parmesan cheese. **6 servings**

PER SERVING: Calories 645; Protein 36 g; Carbohydrate 51 g; Fat 33 g; Cholesterol 180 mg; Sodium 2800 mg

## Pumpkin Ravioli

*A fun twist on an old favorite!*

**1 cup ricotta cheese**
**½ cup canned pumpkin**
**½ teaspoon salt**
**¼ teaspoon ground nutmeg**
**2 cups all-purpose flour**
**½ teaspoon salt**
**¼ cup tomato paste**
**1 tablespoon olive or vegetable oil**
**2 eggs**
**Pumpkin Seed Sauce (right)**

Mix cheese, pumpkin, ½ teaspoon salt and the nutmeg; reserve.

Mix flour and ½ teaspoon salt in large bowl; make well in center. Beat tomato paste, oil and eggs until well blended; pour into well. Stir with fork, gradually bringing flour mixture to center, until dough forms a ball. If dough is too dry, mix in up to 2 tablespoons water. Knead on lightly floured cloth-covered surface, adding flour if dough is sticky, until smooth and elastic, about 5 minutes. Cover; let rest 5 minutes.

Divide dough into 4 equal parts. Roll dough, 1 part at a time, into rectangle, about 12 × 10 inches (keep remaining dough covered). Drop pumpkin mixture by 2 level teaspoonfuls onto half of the rectangle about 1½ inches apart in 2 rows of 4 mounds each. Moisten edges of dough and dough between rows of pumpkin mixture with water. Fold other half of dough up over pumpkin mixture, pressing dough down around mixture. Trim edges with pastry wheel or knife. Cut between rows of filling to make ravioli; press edges with fork to seal. Repeat with remaining dough and pumpkin mixture. Place ravioli on towel; let stand, turning once, until dry, about 30 minutes.

Prepare Pumpkin Seed Sauce. Heat until hot; keep warm. Cook ravioli in 4 quarts boiling

*For round ravioli, cut with 2-inch tortelli cutter or round cookie cutter.*

salted water (2 teaspoons salt) until tender, 10 to 15 minutes; drain carefully. Serve ravioli with sauce. **6 servings**

PER SERVING: Calories 525; Protein 21 g; Carbohydrate 45 g; Fat 29 g; Cholesterol 105 mg; Sodium 830 mg

*Drop pumpkin mixture by 2 level teaspoonfuls onto half of the rectangle about 1½ inches apart in 2 rows of 4 mounds each.*

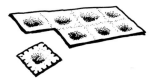

*Cut between rows of filling to make ravioli; press edges with fork to seal.*

### Pumpkin Seed Sauce

**1 cup shelled pumpkin seeds**
**1 small onion, chopped (about ¼ cup)**
**1 slice white bread, torn into small**
  **pieces**
**1 clove garlic, crushed**
**2 tablespoons vegetable oil**
**2 tablespoons canned chopped green**
  **chilies**
**1 can (14 ounces) chicken broth**
**½ cup whipping (heavy) cream**
**Dash of salt**

Cook pumpkin seeds, onion, bread and garlic in oil, stirring frequently, until bread is golden brown. Stir in chilies.

Place mixture in food processor workbowl fitted with steel blade; cover and process until smooth. Stir in broth, whipping cream and salt.

**about 3 cups sauce**

PER SERVING: Calories 225; Protein 10 g; Carbohydrate 7 g; Fat 21 g; Cholesterol 20 mg; Sodium 310 mg

## Baked Spaghetti Sauce

1 pound ground beef
1 large onion, chopped
1 clove garlic, finely chopped
1 can (10¾ ounces) condensed tomato soup
1 can (8 ounces) mushroom stems and pieces, undrained
1 can (8 ounces) tomato sauce
1 can (6 ounces) tomato paste
⅓ cup water
2 teaspoons Italian seasoning
½ teaspoon pepper
Hot cooked spaghetti
Grated Parmesan cheese

Cook and stir ground beef, onion and garlic in 4-quart ovenproof Dutch oven until beef is brown; drain. Stir in remaining ingredients except spaghetti and cheese.

Cover and bake in 350° oven 1 house; stir. Serve over spaghetti; sprinkle with cheese.

**4 servings**

PER SERVING: Calories 615; Protein 35 g; Carbohydrate 74 g; Fat 20 g; Cholesterol 65 mg; Sodium 1570 mg

MICROWAVE DIRECTIONS: Omit water and decrease Italian seasoning to 1 teaspoon. Crumble ground beef into 3-quart microwavable casserole; add onion and garlic. Cover with waxed paper and microwave on high 3 minutes; stir. Cover with waxed paper and microwave until beef is no longer pink, 2 to 3 minutes longer; drain.

Stir in remaining ingredients except spaghetti and cheese. Cover tightly and microwave 5 minutes; stir. Cover tightly and microwave on medium (50%) 15 minutes longer. Serve over spaghetti; sprinkle with cheese.

## Meatballs in Tomato Sauce

1 large onion, chopped (about 1 cup)
1 clove garlic, crushed
1 teaspoon sugar
1 tablespoon chopped fresh or 1 teaspoon dried oregano leaves
¾ teaspoon salt
2 teaspoons chopped fresh or ¾ teaspoon dried basil leaves
1½ teaspoons chopped fresh or ½ teaspoon dried marjoram leaves
1 can (16 ounces) whole tomatoes, undrained
1 can (8 ounces) tomato sauce
Meatballs (below)

Mix all ingredients except Meatballs in 3-quart saucepan; break up tomatoes. Heat to boiling; reduce hat. Cover and simmer, stirring occasionally, 30 minutes.

Prepare Meatballs; drain. Stir Meatballs into tomato mixture. Cover and simmer, stirring occasionally, 30 minutes longer.

### Meatballs

1 pound ground beef
½ cup dry bread crumbs
¼ cup milk
¾ teaspoon salt
½ teaspoon Worcestershire sauce
¼ teaspoon pepper
1 small onion, chopped (about ¼ cup)
1 egg

Heat oven to 400°. Mix all ingredients; shape into twenty 1½-inch balls. Place in ungreased rectangular pan, 13 × 9 × 2 inches. Bake uncovered until done and light brown, 20 to 25 minutes.

**5 servings**

PER SERVING: Calories 300; Protein 21 g; Carbohydrate 20 g; Fat 15 g; Cholesterol 95 mg; Sodium 1200 mg

## Amatriciana Sauce

*This piquant sauce comes from the town of Amatrice, near Rome.*

¼ **pound salt pork**
1 **medium onion, chopped (about ½ cup)**
1 **clove garlic, chopped**
1 **tablespoon olive or vegetable oil**
1 **can (28 ounces) tomatoes**
1 **teaspoon sugar**
¼ **to ½ teaspoon pepper**

Trim rind from salt pork; dice pork. Cook and stir salt pork, onion and garlic in oil in 10-inch skillet until onion is tender; drain. Add tomatoes (with liquid), sugar and pepper; break up tomatoes. Simmer uncovered until mixture is of desired consistency, 30 to 40 minutes.    **4 servings**

PER SERVING: Calories 225; Protein 4 g; Carbohydrate 12 g; Fat 18 g; Cholesterol 15 mg; Sodium 570 mg

## Sugo Sauce

*In Italian, "sugo" means "sauce," and this light tomato sauce is a classic for all types of pasta.*

1 **tablespoon olive oil**
4 **cloves garlic, finely chopped**
1 **small onion, chopped (about ¼ cup)**
2 **cans (28 ounces each) Italian pear-shaped tomatoes, drained**
2 **tablespoons chopped fresh basil leaves**
2 **tablespoons chopped fresh oregano leaves**
½ **teaspoon salt**
½ **teaspoon pepper**

Heat oil in 3-quart saucepan over medium-high heat. Sauté garlic and onion in oil. Place tomatoes in food processor or in blender; cover and process until smooth. Stir tomatoes and remaining ingredients into mixture in saucepan. Heat to boiling; reduce heat. Simmer uncovered 45 minutes, stirring occasionally.

**6 servings**

PER SERVING: Calories 90; Protein 3 g; Carbohydrate 13 g; Fat 3 g; Cholesterol 0 mg; Sodium 610 mg

## Bolognese Sauce

*A classic sauce for pasta from Bologna, Italy.*

2 **tablespoons olive oil**
2 **tablespoons margarine or butter**
2 **medium carrots, chopped (about 1 cup)**
1 **medium onion, chopped (about ½ cup)**
½ **pound bulk Italian sausage**
½ **pound lean ground beef**
½ **cup dry red wine or beef broth**
3 **cans (28 ounces each) Italian pear-shaped tomatoes, drained and chopped**
1 **teaspoon salt**
1 **teaspoon dried oregano leaves**
½ **teaspoon pepper**

Heat oil and margarine in 4-quart Dutch oven over medium-high heat. Sauté carrots and onion in oil mixture. Stir in sausage and ground beef. Cook over medium heat, stirring occasionally, until done; drain. Stir in wine. Heat to boiling; reduce heat. Simmer uncovered until wine is evaporated. Stir in remaining ingredients. Heat to boiling; reduce heat. Cover and simmer 45 minutes, stirring occasionally.    **6 servings**

PER SERVING: Calories 370; Protein 19 g; Carbohydrate 22 g; Fat 23 g; Cholesterol 65 mg; Sodium 1410 mg

**Pesto with Linguine**

## Pesto

*Fresh basil gives pesto a taste of summer. This sauce is delightful on almost any type of pasta.*

1 cup chopped fresh basil leaves
½ cup grated Parmesan cheese
½ cup pine nuts
½ cup chopped fresh parsley
½ cup olive oil
1 teaspoon salt
½ teaspoon pepper
8 cloves garlic

Place all ingredients in food processor or in blender; cover and process until smooth.

**4 servings**

PER SERVING: Calories 415; Protein 7 g; Carbohydrate 9 g; Fat 39 g; Cholesterol 10 mg; Sodium 740 mg

## Mushroom and Brandy Sauce

2 tablespoons margarine or butter
2 cloves garlic, finely chopped
1 small onion, finely chopped (about ¼ cup)
8 ounces fresh mushrooms, thinly sliced
½ cup brandy
4 cups whipping (heavy) cream
½ teaspoon grated nutmeg
½ teaspoon pepper

Heat margarine in 10-inch skillet over medium-high heat. Sauté garlic and onion in margarine. Stir in mushrooms. Sauté 6 minutes. Stir in brandy. Heat to boiling. Carefully ignite. Stir in whipping cream, nutmeg and pepper when flame dies out.* Heat to boiling; reduce heat. Simmer uncovered 20 minutes, stirring frequently, until thickened.

**6 servings**

PER SERVING: Calories 610; Protein 4 g; Carbohydrate 7 g; Fat 63 g; Cholesterol 230 mg; Sodium 90 mg

*To extinguish flame easily, cover with lid.*

## Sauces

Tomato sauces were among the first Italian pasta sauces to catch America's fancy, followed by simple creamy Alfredo-type sauces. Pesto, made from basil, pine nuts and olive oil, has also become a favorite. Now we enjoy a vast array of sauces, flavored with everything from gingerroot and soy sauce to sage, hot peppers, smoked fish and simple, good-quality olive oil. Sauces made without eggs, cheese or cream can be made ahead and frozen for later use. Let the sauce come to room temperature, then cover it tightly, label and freeze.

**Red Clam Sauce with Linguine**

## Red Clam Sauce

¼ cup olive oil
3 cloves garlic, finely chopped
1 can (28 ounces) Italian pear-shaped tomatoes, drained and chopped
1 small red chili, seeded and finely
  chopped
1 pint shucked fresh small clams,
  drained and chopped (reserve liquid)
1 tablespoon chopped fresh parsley
1 teaspoon salt

Heat oil in 10-inch skillet over medium-high heat. Sauté garlic in oil. Stir in tomatoes and chili. Sauté 3 minutes. Stir in clam liquid. Heat to boiling; reduce heat. Simmer uncovered 10 minutes. Stir in clams, parsley and salt. Cover and simmer 30 minutes, stirring occasionally, until clams are tender. **4 servings**

PER SERVING: Calories 225; Protein 11 g; Carbohydrate 12 g; Fat 15 g; Cholesterol 20 mg; Sodium 1140 mg

## White Clam Sauce

1 medium onion, chopped (about ½ cup)
1 clove garlic, finely chopped
3 tablespoons margarine or butter
1 tablespoon all-purpose flour
3 cans (6½ ounces each) minced clams,
  undrained
½ teaspoon salt
1½ teaspoons chopped fresh or ½ teaspoon dried basil leaves
⅛ teaspoon pepper
¼ cup chopped fresh parsley

Cook and stir onion and garlic in margarine in 2-quart saucepan until onion is tender; stir in flour. Add clams (with liquid), salt, basil and pepper. Heat to boiling; reduce heat. Cover and simmer 5 minutes. Stir in parsley. **5 servings**

PER SERVING: Calories 150; Protein 13 g; Carbohydrate 6 g; Fat 8 g; Cholesterol 30 mg; Sodium 590 mg

*Savory Fusilli*

# 2
# Meatless Pasta

## Savory Fusilli

*This is also delicious served cold, as a salad.*

¼ cup olive oil
1 tablespoon capers, drained
3 cloves garlic, finely chopped
2 cans (28 ounces each) Italian pear-shaped tomatoes, drained and chopped
1 small red chili, seeded and chopped
½ cup sliced imported Italian black olives
½ cup sliced green olives
1 tablespoon chopped fresh oregano leaves
1 tablespoon chopped fresh basil leaves
1 package (16 ounces) fusilli (spiral pasta)
Freshly ground pepper

Heat oil in 10-inch skillet over medium-high heat. Sauté capers and garlic in oil. Stir in tomatoes and chili. Heat to boiling; reduce heat. Cover and simmer 20 minutes, stirring occasionally. Stir in olives, oregano and basil. Cover and cook 10 minutes.

Cook fusilli as directed on package; drain. Mix fusilli and tomato mixture. Serve with pepper. **6 servings**

PER SERVING: Calories 435; Protein 12 g; Carbohydrate 63 g; Fat 15 g; Cholesterol 65 mg; Sodium 810 mg

## Mostaccioli with Bell Pepper and Basil

1 green bell pepper, cut into ¼-inch strips
1 onion, sliced and separated into rings
1 clove garlic, crushed
2 tablespoons olive or vegetable oil
1½ cups uncooked mostaccioli
1 medium tomato, coarsely chopped
1 tablespoon chopped fresh or 1 teaspoon dried basil leaves
¼ teaspoon salt
Freshly ground pepper
2 tablespoons grated Romano cheese

Cook and stir green pepper, onion and garlic in oil over medium heat until pepper is tender, about 10 minutes. Cook mostaccioli as directed on package; drain. Stir tomato, basil, salt and pepper into green pepper mixture; heat until hot. Toss with hot mostaccioli; sprinkle with grated cheese. **4 servings**

PER SERVING: Calories 150; Protein 4 g; Carbohydrate 16 g; Fat 8 g; Cholesterol 15 mg; Sodium 190 mg

## Vermicelli and Spinach

**8 ounces uncooked vermicelli**
**6 slices red onion (¼ inch thick), separated into rings**
**2 cloves garlic, crushed**
**2 tablespoons olive or vegetable oil**
**12 ounces spinach, cut crosswise into ½-inch strips (about 12 cups)**
**2 tablespoons lemon juice**
**1 tablespoon chopped fresh or 1 teaspoon dried tarragon leaves**
**¼ teaspoon salt**
**Freshly ground pepper**
**¼ cup crumbled Gorgonzola or blue cheese**

Cook vermicelli as directed on package; drain. Cook and stir onion and garlic in oil in 12-inch skillet over medium heat until onion is almost tender, about 5 minutes. Stir in spinach, lemon juice, tarragon, salt and pepper. Cook and stir until spinach is slightly limp, about 2 minutes. Toss with hot vermicelli; sprinkle with cheese. **8 servings**

PER SERVING: Calories 180; Protein 7 g; Carbohydrate 27 g; Fat 5 g; Cholesterol 5 mg; Sodium 190 mg

## Vermicelli with Fresh Herbs

**¼ cup olive oil**
**2 tablespoons chopped pine nuts**
**1 tablespoon chopped fresh parsley**
**1 tablespoon large capers, drained and chopped**
**2 teaspoons chopped fresh rosemary leaves**
**2 teaspoons chopped fresh sage leaves**
**1 teaspoon chopped fresh basil leaves**
**1 pint cherry tomatoes, cut into fourths**
**1 package (16 ounces) vermicelli**
**Freshly ground pepper**

Mix oil, pine nuts, parsley, capers, rosemary, sage and basil. Stir in tomatoes. Cook vermicelli as directed on package; drain. Mix vermicelli and herb mixture. Serve with pepper.

**6 servings**

PER SERVING: Calories 410; Protein 11 g; Carbohydrate 64 g; Fat 12 g; Cholesterol 0 mg; Sodium 10 mg

# Low-Calorie Pasta

If you love pasta and want to keep your calorie count low, try the following suggestions:

• Mix cooked vegetables with pasta for a hot main dish and raw for a cold salad.

• A 1-cup serving of pasta contains about 200 calories. Substitute ½ cup of cut-up, low-calorie vegetables for ½ cup of the pasta, and you'll cut your calorie count to 120.

• Toss equal parts of cooked spaghetti with cooked spaghetti squash for great flavor.

**Vermicelli with Fresh Herbs**

**Vermicelli with Lemony Green Vegetables**

## Vermicelli with Lemony Green Vegetables

*A great recipe to use up leftover uncooked vegetables.*

1 package (7 ounces) uncooked vermicelli
4 cups mixed bite-size pieces green vegetables (asparagus, broccoli, Chinese pea pods, green beans, zucchini)
¼ cup (½ stick) margarine or butter
1 tablespoon grated lemon peel
½ cup milk
1 package (3 ounces) cream cheese, cut into cubes and softened
½ cup grated Parmesan cheese
Salt and pepper to taste

Cook vermicelli as directed on package; drain. Cook vegetables in margarine in 10-inch skillet over medium heat, stirring frequently, until crisp-tender, about 7 minutes; toss with lemon peel. Remove vegetables; keep warm.

Heat milk and cream cheese in skillet until smooth and creamy; stir in Parmesan cheese, salt and pepper. Toss with hot vermicelli. Serve vegetables over vermicelli and, if desired, with lemon wedges and coarsely ground pepper. **4 servings**

PER SERVING: Calories 475; Protein 16 g; Carbohydrate 49 g; Fat 24 g; Cholesterol 35 mg; Sodium 410 mg

## Angel Hair Pasta in Garlic Sauce

1 package (16 ounces) capellini (angel hair pasta)
¼ cup olive oil
¼ cup chopped fresh parsley
4 cloves garlic, finely chopped
½ cup grated Parmesan cheese
Freshly ground pepper

Cook capellini as directed on package. Meanwhile, heat oil in 10-inch skillet over medium-high heat. Sauté parsley and garlic in oil. Drain capellini and mix with garlic mixture; top with cheese. Serve with pepper. **6 servings**

PER SERVING: Calories 375; Protein 12 g; Carbohydrate 50 g; Fat 14 g; Cholesterol 70 mg; Sodium 140 mg

## Perk Up Pasta

Stir one of the following into cooked pasta for quick flavor:

Fresh or dried herbs
Leftover vegetables
Crisply cooked bacon or fully cooked smoked ham
Water chestnuts and soy sauce
Raisins, citrus peel and juice
Chopped onion, celery and garlic
Chutney and peanuts
Salsa
Barbecue sauce
Pimiento and olives
Chopped green chilies
Shredded cheese

## Ziti with Asparagus Sauce

1½ **pounds fresh asparagus**
2 **tablespoons margarine or butter**
2 **cloves garlic, finely chopped**
1 **leek, thinly sliced**
1 **cup chicken broth**
½ **cup dry white wine or chicken broth**
½ **teaspoon pepper**
1 **package (16 ounces) ziti or other tubu-**
   **lar pasta**
¼ **cup grated Parmesan cheese**

Break off tough ends of asparagus where stalks snap easily. Cover asparagus with cold water. Let stand 1 hour.

Heat margarine in 10-inch skillet over low heat. Stir in garlic and leek. Cover and cook 10 minutes. Stir in chicken broth, wine, pepper and asparagus. Heat to boiling; reduce heat. Cover and simmer about 10 minutes or until asparagus is tender.

Cut tips from 12 stalks of the asparagus; reserve. Place remaining asparagus mixture in food processor or in blender; cover and process until smooth.

Cook ziti as directed on package; drain. Mix ziti and sauce; top with asparagus tips and cheese. **6 servings**

PER SERVING: Calories 355; Protein 15 g; Carbohydrate 56 g; Fat 8 g; Cholesterol 80 mg; Sodium 240 mg

## Penne with Radicchio

*Radicchio is a type of chicory with reddish leaves. If it's not available, red cabbage can be substituted.*

2 **tablespoons olive oil**
2 **tablespoons margarine or butter**
1 **medium onion, thinly sliced**
1 **head radicchio, cut into ¼-inch strips,**
   **or ¼ cup red cabbage cut into ¼-inch**
   **shreds**
½ **cup dry white wine or chicken broth**
1 **cup whipping (heavy) cream**
½ **teaspoon pepper**
1 **package (16 ounces) penne**
½ **cup freshly grated Parmesan cheese**

Heat oil and margarine in 10-inch skillet over medium-high heat. Sauté onion in oil mixture. Stir in radicchio. Cover and cook over low heat 5 minutes or until tender. Stir in wine. Cook uncovered until liquid is evaporated. Stir in whipping cream and pepper. Heat to boiling; reduce heat. Simmer uncovered 30 minutes, stirring frequently, until thickened.

Cook penne as directed on package; drain. Mix penne and radicchio mixture; top with cheese. **6 servings**

PER SERVING: Calories 530; Protein 15 g; Carbohydrate 55 g; Fat 28 g; Cholesterol 135 mg; Sodium 190 mg

**Penne with Radicchio**

## Macaroni and Cheese

**1 package (7 ounces) uncooked elbow, rotini or ziti macaroni (about 2 cups)**
**2 tablespoons margarine or butter**
**1 small onion, chopped (about ¼ cup)**
**2 tablespoons all-purpose flour**
**½ teaspoon salt**
**¼ teaspoon pepper**
**2 cups milk**
**8 ounces sharp process American or Swiss cheese, process American cheese loaf or process cheese spread loaf, cut into ½-inch cubes, or shredded Cheddar cheese**

Heat oven to 375°. Cook macaroni as directed on package. Heat margarine in 3-quart saucepan over medium heat. Cook onion in margarine about 3 minutes. Stir in flour, salt and pepper. Cook, stirring constantly, until mixture is bubbly; remove from heat. Stir in milk. Heat to boiling, stirring constantly. Boil and stir 1 minute; remove from heat. Stir in cheese until melted. Add macaroni and stir until coated. Pour into ungreased 1½-quart casserole. Bake about 30 minutes or until bubbly and light brown. **6 servings**

---

MICROWAVE DIRECTIONS: Mix macaroni, 2 cups hot water, the margarine, onion, salt and pepper in 2-quart microwavable casserole. Cover tightly and microwave on high 5 minutes; stir. Cover tightly and microwave on medium (50%) 4 to 6 minutes or until boiling. Reduce milk to 1¼ cups. Stir in remaining ingredients. Cover tightly and microwave on high 5 to 8 minutes, stirring every 3 minutes, until mixture is bubbly and macaroni is tender. Let stand uncovered 5 minutes before serving.

PER SERVING: Calories 355; Protein 18 g; Carbohydrate 31 g; Fat 17 g; Cholesterol 75 mg; Sodium 370 mg

## Macaroni and Cheese with Green Chilies

*Green chilies add zest to familiar macaroni and cheese.*

**3 cups uncooked shell macaroni (about 12 ounces)**
**½ cup shredded Cheddar cheese (2 ounces)**
**½ cup sliced ripe olives**
**1 cup half-and-half**
**½ teaspoon salt**
**½ cup chopped fresh mild green chilies or 1 can (4 ounces) chopped green chilies, drained**
**½ cup chopped red bell pepper or 1 jar (2 ounces) diced pimientos, drained**

Cook macaroni as directed on package; drain. Stir in remaining ingredients. Cook over low heat, stirring occasionally, until cheese is melted and sauce is hot, about 5 minutes.

**6 servings**

PER SERVING: Calories 325; Protein 11 g; Carbohydrate 48 g; Fat 10 g; Cholesterol 25 mg; Sodium 350 mg

# Macaroni con Queso

**Chile con Queso (below)**
**4 ounces uncooked elbow macaroni or**
**macaroni shells (about 1 cup)**
**1 large tomato, chopped (about 1 cup)**
**1 tablespoon chopped fresh cilantro**
**1 cup shredded Cheddar or Monterey**
**Jack cheese (4 ounces)**
**¼ cup crushed tortilla chips**

Heat oven to 375°. Prepare Chile con Queso. Cook macaroni as directed on package; drain. Mix macaroni, Chile con Queso, tomato and cilantro in ungreased 1½-quart casserole. Sprinkle with cheese and tortilla chips. Bake uncovered about 30 minutes or until hot and bubbly.

**4 servings**

PER SERVING: Calories 395; Protein 19 g; Carbohydrate 28 g; Fat 23 g; Cholesterol 70 mg; Sodium 700 mg

## Chile con Queso

**1 cup shredded Cheddar or Monterey**
**jack cheese (4 ounces)**
**1 or 2 jalapeño chilies, seeded and finely**
**chopped**
**½ cup milk**
**¼ cup half-and-half**
**2 tablespoons finely chopped onion**
**2 teaspoons ground cumin**
**½ teaspoon salt**

Heat all ingredients over low heat, stirring constantly, until cheese is melted.

# Three-Cheese Tortellini

*A quick dinner for a busy night!*

**1 package (7 ounces) dried cheese-filled**
**tortellini**
**¼ cup (½ stick) margarine or butter**
**½ cup chopped green bell pepper**
**2 shallots, finely chopped**
**1 clove garlic, finely chopped**
**¼ cup all-purpose flour**
**¼ teaspoon pepper**
**1¾ cups milk**
**½ cup shredded mozzarella cheese**
**(2 ounces)**
**½ cup shredded Swiss cheese (2 ounces)**
**¼ cup grated Parmesan or Romano**
**cheese**

Cook tortellini as directed on package; drain. Heat margarine in 3-quart saucepan over medium heat. Cook bell pepper, shallots and garlic in margarine about 3 minutes. Stir in flour and pepper. Cook, stirring constantly, until mixture is bubbly; remove form heat. Stir in milk. Heat to boiling, stirring constantly. Boil and stir 1 minute; remove from heat. Stir in mozzarella and Swiss cheeses until melted. Add tortellini and stir until coated. Sprinkle with Parmesan cheese.

**5 servings**

PER SERVING: Calories 390; Protein 16 g; Carbohydrate 41 g; Fat 18 g; Cholesterol 30 mg; Sodium 300 mg

# Vegetable Lasagne

*This fresh-tasting lasagne is a great way to serve vegetables to fussy eaters.*

**White Sauce (right)**
**1 package (10 ounces) frozen chopped spinach**
**2 cups creamed cottage cheese**
**½ cup grated Parmesan cheese**
**1 tablespoon chopped fresh or 1 teaspoon dried basil leaves**
**1½ teaspoons chopped fresh or ½ teaspoon dried oregano leaves**
**¼ teaspoon pepper**
**12 lasagne noodles, cooked and drained**
**1½ cups shredded mozzarella cheese**
**1 can (8 ounces) mushroom stems and pieces, drained and coarsely chopped**
**2 medium carrots, coarsely shredded**
**1 medium onion, chopped (about ½ cup)**
**1 medium green bell pepper, chopped (about 1 cup)**

Heat oven to 350°. Prepare White Sauce. Rinse frozen spinach under running cold water to separate. Drain; pat dry with paper towels. Mix spinach, cottage cheese, ¼ cup of the Parmesan cheese, the basil, oregano and pepper. Arrange 4 noodles in ungreased 13 × 9 × 2-inch baking dish. Top with half of the cheese mixture, ½ cup of the mozzarella cheese and 4 noodles. Layer mushrooms, carrots, onion and green pepper on noodles. Spread half of the White Sauce over top; sprinkle with ½ cup of the mozzarella cheese. Top with remaining noodles, cheese mixture, White Sauce and mozzarella cheese; sprinkle with remaining ¼ cup Parmesan cheese.

Bake uncovered until hot and bubbly, about 35 minutes. Let stand 10 minutes before cutting. **8 servings**

PER SERVING: Calories 420; Protein 24 g; Carbohydrate 40 g; Fat 18 g; Cholesterol 30 mg; Sodium 970 mg

## White Sauce

**⅓ cup margarine or butter**
**⅓ cup all-purpose flour**
**1 teaspoon salt**
**⅛ teaspoon ground nutmeg**
**3 cups milk**

Heat margarine in 1-quart saucepan over low heat until melted. Stir in flour, salt and nutmeg.

Cook over low heat, stirring constantly, until bubbly; remove from heat. Stir in milk. Heat to boiling, stirring constantly. Boil and stir 1 minute; cover and keep warm. (If sauce thickens, beat in small amount of milk.)

## Cheesy Lasagne

½ cup (1 stick) margarine or butter
½ cup all-purpose flour
½ teaspoon salt
4 cups milk
1 cup shredded Swiss cheese (4 ounces)
1 cup shredded mozzarella cheese
  (4 ounces)
½ cup grated Parmesan cheese
2 cups small-curd creamed cottage
  cheese
¼ cup chopped fresh parsley
1 teaspoon dried basil leaves
½ teaspoon dried oregano leaves
2 cloves garlic, crushed
12 uncooked lasagne noodles
½ cup grated Parmesan cheese

Heat oven to 350°. Heat margarine in 2-quart saucepan until melted. Stir in flour and salt until blended. Cook over low heat, stirring constantly, until smooth and bubbly; remove from heat. Stir in milk. Heat to boiling, stirring constantly. Boil and stir 1 minute. Stir in Swiss cheese, mozzarella cheese and ½ cup Parmesan cheese. Cook over low heat, stirring constantly, until cheeses are melted. Mix cottage cheese, parsley, basil, oregano and garlic.

Spread one-fourth of the hot cheese mixture in ungreased rectangular baking dish, 13 × 9 × 2 inches. Top with 4 uncooked noodles. Spread 1 cup of the cottage cheese mixture over noodles; spread with one-fourth of the hot cheese mixture. Repeat with 4 noodles, the remaining cottage cheese mixture, one-fourth of the hot cheese mixture, the remaining noodles and remaining hot cheese mixture. Sprinkle with ½ cup Parmesan cheese. Bake uncovered 35 to 40 minutes or until noodles are done. Let stand 10 minutes before cutting.          **12 servings**

PER SERVING: Calories 325; Protein 18 g; Carbohydrate 24 g; Fat 17 g; Cholesterol 50 mg; Sodium 560 mg

## Noodles Romanoff

*These rich noodles come from Eastern Europe and Russia. Garnish with poppy seed for added flavor.*

8 ounces uncooked wide noodles
2 cups sour cream
¼ cup grated Parmesan cheese
1 tablespoon chopped fresh chives
½ teaspoon salt
⅛ teaspoon pepper
1 large clove garlic, crushed
2 tablespoons margarine or butter
¼ cup grated Parmesan cheese

Cook noodles as directed on package; drain. Mix sour cream, ¼ cup cheese, the chives, salt, pepper and garlic. Stir margarine into hot noodles. Stir in sour cream mixture. Place on warm platter. Sprinkle with ¼ cup cheese.

**8 servings**

PER SERVING: Calories 210; Protein 5 g; Carbohydrate 9 g; Fat 17 g; Cholesterol 40 mg; Sodium 295 mg

# Manicotti

*The secret to tender, evenly cooked shells is to make sure sauce covers the bottom of the pan and the shells.*

- **1 large tomato, chopped (about 1 cup)**
- **1 tablespoon chopped fresh or 1 teaspoon dried basil leaves**
- **2 cans (15 ounces each) tomato sauce**
- **2 cups creamed cottage cheese**
- **¼ cup grated Parmesan cheese**
- **1 clove garlic, finely chopped**
- **1 teaspoon chopped fresh or ½ teaspoon dried thyme leaves**
- **1 small onion, chopped (about ¼ cup)**
- **2 eggs**
- **1 package (10 ounces) frozen chopped spinach, thawed and drained**
- **1 package (8 ounces) manicotti shells (14 shells)**
- **1 cup shredded mozzarella cheese (4 ounces)**

Heat oven to 350°. Grease rectangular pan or baking dish, 13 × 9 × 2 inches. Mix tomato, basil and tomato sauce. Spread 1½ cups evenly in pan. Mix remaining ingredients except manicotti and mozzarella cheese. Fill uncooked manicotti shells with spinach mixture. Arrange in pan. Pour remaining tomato sauce mixture over manicotti. Cover and bake about 1½ hours or until manicotti shells are tender. Sprinkle with mozzarella cheese. **7 servings**

PER SERVING: Calories 325; Protein 22 g; Carbohydrate 37 g; Fat 11 g; Cholesterol 135 g; Sodium 1090 mg

# Tortellini in Balsamic Vinaigrette

- **1 package (7 ounces) uncooked tricolor cheese tortellini**
- **Balsamic Vinaigrette (below)**
- **1 medium carrot, sliced**
- **2 cups broccoli flowerets**
- **2 green onions (with tops), sliced**

Cook tortellini as directed on package; drain. Rinse with cold water; drain.

Prepare Balsamic Vinaigrette in large bowl. Stir in remaining ingredients except tortellini. Stir in tortellini. **4 servings**

PER SERVING: Calories 215; Protein 9 g; Carbohydrate 18 g; Fat 12 g; Cholesterol 70 mg; Sodium 210 mg

## Balsamic Vinaigrette

- **¼ cup balsamic or cider vinegar**
- **2 tablespoons olive or vegetable oil**
- **1 tablespoon chopped fresh or 1 teaspoon dried basil leaves**
- **¼ teaspoon paprika**
- **⅛ teaspoon salt**
- **1 clove garlic, crushed**

Mix all ingredients.

*Tortellini in Balsamic Vinaigrette*

## Tortellini Soup

2 cloves garlic, finely chopped
2 medium stalks celery, chopped
1 small onion, chopped (about ¼ cup)
1 medium carrot, chopped
3 tablespoons margarine or butter
8 cups chicken broth
4 cups water
2 packages (10 ounces each) dried
  cheese-filled tortellini
2 tablespoons chopped fresh parsley
½ teaspoon pepper
1 teaspoon grated nutmeg
Grated Parmesan cheese

Cover and cook garlic, celery, onion and carrot in margarine in 6-quart Dutch oven over medium-low heat 10 minutes. Stir in chicken broth and water. Heat to boiling; reduce heat. Stir in tortellini; cover and simmer 20 minutes, stirring occasionally, or until tortellini are tender.

Stir in parsley, pepper and nutmeg. Cover and cook 10 minutes. Top each serving with cheese. **8 servings**

PER SERVING: Calories 265; Protein 16 g; Carbohydrate 21 g; Fat 13 g; Cholesterol 115 mg; Sodium 1020 mg

## Chili Beans and Pasta

*A hearty dish, perfect for a cold-weather dinner.*

4 cups water
1 pound dried great northern beans
1 medium onion, chopped (about ½ cup)
2 cloves garlic, finely chopped
1 tablespoon chili powder
1 teaspoon salt
1 can (28 ounces) whole tomatoes,
  undrained
1 can (4 ounces) chopped green chilies,
  undrained
1 cup uncooked small macaroni shells
  (about 3 ounces)
1 cup shredded Monterey Jack or Cheddar cheese (4 ounces)
½ cup sliced green onions (with tops)

Heat water and beans to boiling in Dutch oven. Boil 2 minutes; remove form heat. Cover and let stand 1 hour.

Add enough water to beans to cover if necessary. Add onion, garlic, chili powder and salt. Heat to boiling; reduce heat. Cover and simmer about 1 hour 30 minutes or until beans are tender (do not boil or beans will burst).

Stir in tomatoes, chilies and macaroni; break up tomatoes. Heat to boiling; reduce heat. Cover and simmer about 15 minutes or until macaroni is tender. Sprinkle each serving with cheese and green onions. **8 servings**

PER SERVING: Calories 315; Protein 18 g; Carbohydrate 49 g; Fat 6 g; Cholesterol 15 mg; Sodium 54 mg

## Tomato-Pasta Salad

1 package (7 ounces) macaroni shells
2 medium tomatoes, chopped (about 2 cups)
2 green onions (with tops), chopped (about 2 tablespoons)
2 cloves garlic, finely chopped
1/4 cup chopped fresh parsley
2 tablespoons olive or vegetable oil
1/2 teaspoon salt
1 1/2 teaspoons chopped fresh or 1/2 teaspoon dried basil leaves
1/8 teaspoon coarsely cracked pepper

Cook macaroni as directed on package. Rinse in cold water and drain. Stir in tomatoes, onions, garlic, parsley, oil, salt, basil and pepper. Cover and refrigerate about 2 hours or until chilled. **6 servings**

PER SERVING: Calories 145; Protein 3 g; Carbohydrate 22 g; Fat 5 g; Cholesterol 0 mg; Sodium 190 mg

## Pesto-Macaroni Salad

*While homemade pesto adds wonderful flavor, pesto from the store is delicious in this salad too.*

3 cups uncooked medium shell macaroni
1 tablespoon olive or vegetable oil
1 cup Pesto (page 13) or 1 container (8 ounces) pesto
1/2 cup small pitted ripe olives
1/4 cup white wine vinegar
4 Italian plum tomatoes, each cut into 4 wedges
4 cups coarsely shredded spinach
Grated Parmesan cheese, if desired

Cook macaroni as directed on package. Rinse in cold water and drain; toss with oil. Mix pesto, olives, vinegar and tomatoes in large bowl. Arrange 2 cups macaroni and 2 cups spinach on olive mixture; repeat with remaining macaroni and spinach. Cover and refrigerate at least 2 hours. Toss and sprinkle with cheese.

**6 servings**

PER SERVING: Calories 500; Protein 12 g; Carbohydrate 48 g; Fat 30 g; Cholesterol 5 mg; Sodium 275 mg

**Tarragon with Chicken Pasta**

# 3

# Poultry and Pasta

## Tarragon and Chicken Pasta

*Tarragon with its distinctive, aniselike flavor is a marvelous seasoning for chicken.*

**1 cup uncooked spiral macaroni (about 4 ounces)**
**2 cups sliced mushrooms (about 5 ounces)**
**1 cup broccoli flowerets**
**1 cup thinly sliced carrots (about 2 large)**
**1 cup skim milk**
**1 tablespoon cornstarch**
**2 teaspoons chopped fresh or ½ teaspoon dried tarragon leaves**
**¼ teaspoon salt**
**1 clove garlic, finely chopped**
**2 cups shredded spinach or romaine lettuce (about 3 ounces)**
**1½ cups cut-up cooked chicken or turkey (about 8 ounces)**
**½ cup shredded Swiss cheese (2 ounces)**

Cook macaroni as directed on package—except add mushrooms, broccoli and carrots during last 4 minutes of cooking; drain.

Mix milk, cornstarch, tarragon, salt and garlic in 1½-quart saucepan. Cook over medium heat 4 minutes, stirring constantly, until mixture thickens and boils. Stir in remaining ingredients until cheese is melted and spinach is wilted. Toss with macaroni mixture.     **4 servings**

PER SERVING: Calories 315; Protein 27 g; Carbohydrate 35 g; Fat 7 g; Cholesterol 55 mg; Sodium 280 mg

## Flavored Pasta Water

Salting the cooking water is optional and not necessary for the proper cooking of pasta. You might like to add a tablespoon of dried herbs or lemon juice to the water for a slightly different flavor. Try one of the following herbs:
- Oregano
- Basil
- Rosemary
- Dill
- Tarragon

## Chicken-Basil Noodles

2 teaspoons olive or vegetable oil
½ cup finely chopped onion (about 1
    medium)
1 clove garlic, finely chopped
2½ cups chopped tomatoes (about 3
    medium)
2 cups cubed cooked chicken or turkey
¼ cup chopped fresh or 1 tablespoon
    dried basil leaves
½ teaspoon salt
⅛ teaspoon red pepper sauce
4 ounces uncooked noodles (about 2
    cups)

Heat oil in 10-inch nonstick skillet over medium-high heat. Cook onion and garlic in oil until softened. Stir in remaining ingredients except noodles; reduce heat to medium. Cover and cook about 5 minutes, stirring frequently, until mixture is hot and tomatoes are soft. Cook noodles as directed on package; drain. Serve chicken mixture over noodles.                    **4 servings**

PER SERVING: Calories 280; Protein 24 g; Carbohydrate 28 g; Fat 8 g; Cholesterol 60 mg; Sodium 330 mg

## Penne with Vodka Sauce

*Brandy or grappa, an Italian brandy, can be substituted for the vodka.*

3 tablespoons margarine or butter
1 tablespoon olive oil
2 cloves garlic, finely chopped
1 small onion, chopped (about ¼ cup)
¼ cup chopped prosciutto or fully
    cooked Virginia ham
2 skinless boneless chicken breast
    halves, cut into ½-inch pieces
½ cup vodka
½ cup whipping (heavy) cream
½ cup sliced imported Italian black olives
1 tablespoon chopped fresh parsley
½ teaspoon pepper
1 package (16 ounces) penne or
    mostaccioli
2 tablespoons grated Parmesan cheese

Heat margarine and oil in 10-inch skillet over medium-high heat. Sauté garlic and onion in margarine mixture. Stir in prosciutto and chicken. Cook, stirring occasionally, until chicken is brown. Stir in vodka. Heat over high heat until hot.

Carefully ignite. Stir in whipping cream, olives, parsley and pepper when flame dies out.* Heat to boiling; reduce heat. Simmer uncovered 30 minutes, stirring frequently, until thickened.

Cook penne as directed on package. Mix penne and cream mixture; top with cheese.

**6 servings**

PER SERVING: Calories 485; Protein 21 g; Carbohydrate 51 g; Fat 22 g; Cholesterol 135 mg; Sodium 300 mg

*To extinguish flame easily, cover with lid.

# Thai Chicken with Cellophane Noodles

- 1 package (3¾ ounces) cellophane noodles
- 1 pound skinless boneless chicken breast halves or thighs
- 2 tablespoons vegetable oil
- 1 cup thinly sliced carrots
- 4 serrano chilies, seeded and finely chopped
- 2 cups shredded Chinese cabbage
- 1 cup diagonally sliced celery
- 3 green onions (with tops), cut into 2-inch pieces
- ⅓ cup fish sauce or soy sauce
- 2 teaspoons finely shredded lime peel

Cover noodles with cold water. Let stand 20 minutes; drain. Cut into 3- to 4-inch pieces. Cut chicken breast halves into thin slices.

Heat wok or 12-inch skillet until hot. Add oil and tilt wok to coat side. Add chicken, carrots and chilies. Stir-fry about 4 minutes or until chicken is white. Remove from wok.

Add cabbage, celery and onions. Stir-fry 1 minute. Stir in chicken, noodles and remaining ingredients. Stir-fry about 1 minute or until mixture is hot. **4 servings**

PER SERVING: Calories 205; Protein 21 g; Carbohydrate 12 g; Fat 9 g; Cholesterol 45 mg; Sodium 1465 mg

# Linguine with Chicken and Artichoke Hearts

- 1 jar (6 ounces) marinated artichoke hearts
- 1 tablespoon olive or vegetable oil
- ½ cup coarsely chopped onion (about 1 medium)
- 2 cups cut-up cooked chicken or turkey (about 10 ounces)
- 1 cup frozen green peas
- 2 ounces sliced fully cooked extra-lean smoked ham, cut into ¼-inch strips (about ½ cup)*
- 1 tablespoon chopped fresh or 1 teaspoon dried oregano leaves
- ¼ teaspoon pepper
- 1 container (8 ounces) low-fat sour cream (1 cup)
- 6 ounces uncooked linguine or spaghetti

Drain liquid from artichoke hearts into 10-inch skillet. Cut artichoke hearts into halves and reserve. Add oil to artichoke liquid. Cook onion in oil mixture, stirring occasionally, until softened.

Stir artichoke hearts, chicken, peas, ham, oregano and pepper into onion mixture. Cook, stirring occasionally, until hot; remove from heat. Stir in sour cream. Cover and keep warm. Cook linguine as directed on package; drain. Toss linguine with sauce. **4 servings**

PER SERVING: Calories 350; Protein 28 g; Carbohydrate 42 g; Fat 9 g; Cholesterol 65 mg; Sodium 260 mg

*6 slices bacon, crisply cooked and crumbled, can be substituted for the ham.

## Chicken-Pasta Primavera

1 cup chopped broccoli
1/3 cup chopped onion (about 1 medium)
2 cloves garlic, finely chopped
1 carrot, cut into very thin strips
3 tablespoons vegetable oil
2 cups cut-up cooked chicken
1/2 teaspoon salt
2 medium tomatoes, chopped (about 2
   cups)
4 cups hot cooked macaroni shells
1/3 cup freshly grated Parmesan cheese
2 tablespoons chopped fresh parsley

Cook the broccoli, onion, garlic and the carrot in oil in 10-inch skillet over medium heat about 10 minutes, stirring frequently, until broccoli is crisp-tender. Stir in chicken, salt and tomatoes. Heat about 3 minutes or just until chicken is hot.

Spoon chicken mixture over macaroni. Sprinkle with cheese and parsley.          **6 servings**

PER SERVING: Calories 320;  Protein 20 g;  Carbohydrate 32 g; Fat 12 g; Cholesterol 40 mg; Sodium 310 mg

## Pasta Shells with Chicken and Broccoli

*For variety, try different shapes and flavors of pasta. Use similar size pastas, so cooking time is consistent.*

6 ounces uncooked macaroni shells or
   wheels
1 cup chopped broccoli
1/3 cup chopped onion (about 1 medium)
2 cloves garlic, finely chopped
1 carrot, cut into very thin strips
2 tablespoons vegetable oil
2 cups cut-up cooked chicken or turkey
1 teaspoon salt
2 large tomatoes, chopped (about 2
   cups)
1/3 cup grated Parmesan cheese
2 tablespoons chopped fresh parsley

Cook macaroni as directed on package; drain. Cook broccoli, onion, garlic and carrot in oil in 10-inch skillet over medium heat about 10 minutes, stirring occasionally, until broccoli is crisp-tender.

Stir in chicken, salt and tomatoes. Cook uncovered about 3 minutes or just until chicken is hot. Spoon over macaroni. Sprinkle with cheese and parsley.          **6 servings**

PER SERVING: Calories 325;  Protein 20 g;  Carbohydrate 33 g; Fat 12 g; Cholesterol 40 mg; Sodium 490 mg

*Pasta Shells with Chicken and Broccoli*

## Turkey-Pasta Primavera

**6 ounces uncooked spaghetti or
fettuccine**
**1 cup chopped broccoli**
**⅓ cup chopped onion**
**2 cloves garlic, finely chopped**
**½ cup julienne strips carrot (about 1
medium)**
**1 tablespoon vegetable oil**
**2 cups cut-up cooked turkey or chicken**
**1 teaspoon salt**
**2 cups chopped tomatoes (about 2 large)**
**⅓ cup freshly grated Parmesan cheese**
**2 tablespoons chopped fresh parsley**

Cook spaghetti as directed on package; drain.

Cook broccoli, onion, garlic and carrot in oil in
10-inch nonstick skillet over medium heat about
10 minutes, stirring occasionally, until broccoli is
crisp-tender.

Stir in turkey, salt and tomatoes. Heat about
3 minutes or just until turkey is hot. Spoon
over spaghetti. Sprinkle with cheese and
parsley.                                **6 servings**

PER SERVING: Calories 300; Protein 21 g; Carbohydrate 34 g; Fat 9 g; Cholesterol 75 mg; Sodium 670 mg

## Turkey Pasta with Pesto

*Use a flavorful olive oil to make this varia-
tion of pesto. Calories have been cut dra-
matically here, but the wonderful,
distinctive flavor remains.*

**Pesto (below)**
**2 cups uncooked rigatoni macaroni
(about 4 ounces)**
**2 cups ¼-inch zucchini slices (about 2
medium)**
**⅓ cup chopped onion**
**1 medium carrot, cut into julienne strips**
**2 teaspoons olive or vegetable oil**
**3 cups cut-up cooked turkey or chicken**

Prepare Pesto. Cook macaroni as directed on
package; drain.

Cook and stir zucchini, onion and carrot in oil in
10-inch nonstick skillet over medium heat until
zucchini is crisp-tender, 3 to 4 minutes. Stir in
turkey; heat just until turkey is hot, about 3 minutes. Stir in macaroni and Pesto; toss until well
coated. Heat until hot.                 **6 servings**

PER SERVING: Calories 315; Protein 29 g; Carbohydrate 22 g; Fat 12 g; Cholesterol 60 mg; Sodium 125 mg

### Pesto

**2 tablespoons olive oil**
**1 tablespoon nonfat plain yogurt**
**2 teaspoons lemon juice**
**¼ cup grated Parmesan cheese**
**1 tablespoon pine nuts**
**2 to 3 cloves garlic**
**1 cup firmly packed fresh basil leaves**

Place all ingredients in blender container in
order listed. Cover and blend on medium speed,
stopping blender occasionally to scrape sides,
until almost smooth, about 2 minutes.

# Curried Turkey Spaghetti

*Curry is a catch-all term used to refer to many types of spicy sauces, all of which have curry powder as a dominant ingredient. To vary this curry, try spinach or whole wheat pasta.*

½ pound ground turkey or lean ground beef
½ cup chopped onion (about 1 medium)
1 clove garlic, finely chopped
¾ cup chopped unpared tart eating apple (about 1 medium)
¼ cup chopped fresh parsley
1½ teaspoons curry powder
½ teaspoon ground cumin
⅛ teaspoon ground red pepper (cayenne)
¼ cup unsweetened apple juice
1 can (16 ounces) whole tomatoes, undrained
6 ounces uncooked spaghetti
2 tablespoons chopped dry roasted peanuts

Cook ground turkey, onion and garlic in 10-inch skillet over medium heat, stirring frequently, until turkey is no longer pink; drain. Stir in remaining ingredients except spaghetti and peanuts; break up tomatoes. Heat to boiling; reduce heat. Simmer uncovered about 5 minutes or until apple is tender, stirring occasionally.

Cook spaghetti as directed on package; drain. Serve sauce over spaghetti. Sprinkle with peanuts. **4 servings**

PER SERVING: Calories 350; Protein 21 g; Carbohydrate 50 g; Fat 8 g; Cholesterol 35 mg; Sodium 260 mg

# Chicken Tetrazzini

¼ cup (½ stick) margarine or butter
¼ cup all-purpose flour
½ teaspoon salt
¼ teaspoon pepper
1 cup chicken broth
1 cup whipping (heavy) cream
2 tablespoons sherry or chicken broth
1 package (7 ounces) spaghetti, cooked and drained
2 cups cubed cooked chicken
1 jar (2.5 ounces) sliced mushrooms, drained
½ cup grated Parmesan cheese

Heat oven to 350°. Heat margarine in 3-quart saucepan over low heat until melted. Stir in flour, salt and pepper until blended. Cook over low heat, stirring constantly, until smooth and bubbly; remove from heat. Stir in broth and whipping cream. Heat to boiling, stirring constantly. Boil and stir 1 minute. Stir in sherry, spaghetti, chicken and mushrooms. Pour into ungreased 2-quart casserole. Sprinkle with cheese. Bake uncovered 30 minutes or until bubbly. To brown top, place briefly under broiler. **6 servings**

PER SERVING: Calories 480; Protein 23 g; Carbohydrate 30 g; Fat 29 g; Cholesterol 130 mg; Sodium 590 mg

## Turkey and Ham Tetrazzini

*To toast almonds, heat oven to 350°. Bake in ungreased pan about 10 minutes, stirring occasionally, until golden brown.*

**1 package (7 ounces) spaghetti**
**1 can (10¾ ounces) condensed cream of mushroom soup**
**1 can (10¾ ounces) condensed cream of chicken soup**
**¾ cup milk**
**2 tablespoons dry white wine or chicken broth**
**2 cups cut-up cooked turkey or chicken**
**½ cup cut-up fully cooked smoked ham**
**1 small green bell pepper, chopped (about ½ cup)**
**½ cup halved pitted ripe olives**
**½ cup grated Parmesan cheese**
**¼ cup slivered almonds, toasted**

Heat oven to 375°. Cook spaghetti as directed on package; rinse with cold water and drain. Mix soups, milk and wine in ungreased 2-quart casserole. Stir in spaghetti, turkey, ham, bell pepper and olives. Sprinkle with cheese. Bake uncovered about 35 minutes or until hot and bubbly. Sprinkle with almonds. **6 servings**

PER SERVING: Calories 395; Protein 24 g; Carbohydrate 31 g; Fat 19 g; Cholesterol 55 mg; Sodium 1090 mg

## Chicken Noodle Soup

*One of the all-time favorite comfort foods.*

**Chicken and Broth (page 41)**
**2 medium carrots, sliced (about 1 cup)**
**2 medium stalks celery, sliced (about 1 cup)**
**1 small onion, chopped (about ¼ cup)**
**1 tablespoon instant chicken bouillon**
**1 cup uncooked medium noodles (about 2 ounces)**

Prepare Chicken and Broth. Reserve cut-up chicken. Add enough water to broth to measure 5 cups. Heat broth, carrots, celery, onion and bouillon (dry) granules to boiling; reduce heat. Cover and simmer about 15 minutes or until carrots are tender. Stir in noodles and chicken. Heat to boiling; reduce heat. Simmer uncovered 7 to 10 minutes or until noodles are tender. Sprinkle with chopped parsley if desired.

**6 servings**

PER SERVING: Calories 295; Protein 31 g; Carbohydrate 7 g; Fat 15 g; Cholesterol 90 mg; Sodium 670 mg

# Chicken and Broth

**3- to 3½-pound broiler-fryer chicken, cut up***
**4½ cups cold water**
**1 teaspoon salt**
**½ teaspoon pepper**
**1 stalk celery with leaves, cut up**
**1 medium carrot, cut up**
**1 small onion, cut up**
**1 sprig parsley**

Remove any excess fat from chicken. Place chicken, giblets (except liver) and neck in Dutch oven. Add remaining ingredients and heat to boiling. Skim foam from broth; reduce heat. Cover and simmer about 45 minutes or until juices of chicken run clear.

Remove chicken from broth. Cool chicken about 10 minutes or just until cool enough to handle. Strain broth through cheesecloth-lined sieve; discard vegetables. Remove skin and bones from chicken. Cut up chicken. Skim fat from broth. Cover and refrigerate broth and chicken in separate containers no longer than 24 hours, or freeze for future use.

**about 3 cups cooked chicken; about 3 cups broth**

PER SERVING (CHICKEN): Calories 335; Protein 38 g; Carbohydrate 0 g; Fat 19 g; Cholesterol 125 mg; Sodium 115 mg
PER SERVING (BROTH): Calories 40; Protein 5 g; Carbohydrate 1 g; Fat 1 g; Cholesterol 0 mg; Sodium 775 mg

*3 to 3½ pounds chicken necks, backs and giblets (except liver) can be used to make broth.*

# Turkey Tortellini Soup

**1 package (7 ounces) dried cheese-filled tortellini**
**2¼ cups water**
**2 tablespoons rice wine vinegar or white wine vinegar**
**2 tablespoons soy sauce**
**1 can (10¾ ounces) condensed chicken broth**
**1 to 2 tablespoons finely chopped gingerroot or 1 to 2 teaspoons ground ginger**
**2 cups sliced bok choy**
**2 cups cut-up cooked turkey (about 10 ounces)**
**2 green onions (with tops), sliced**
**1 cup enoki mushrooms**

Cook tortellini as directed on package; drain. Heat water, vinegar, soy sauce, chicken broth and gingerroot to boiling in 3-quart saucepan; reduce heat. Stir in bok choy stems (reserve leaves), turkey and onions. Simmer 15 minutes. Stir in bok choy leaves and mushrooms. Simmer just until leaves are wilted. **4 servings**

PER SERVING: Calories 350; Protein 32 g; Carbohydrate 42 g; Fat 5 g; Cholesterol 55 mg; Sodium 1070 mg

*Chicken-Pasta Salad*

## Chicken-Pasta Salad

*Cooking the pea pods with the pasta makes this salad even easier and quicker.*

1 package (6 ounces) frozen pea pods
1 package (5 ounces) spiral macaroni
⅓ cup mayonnaise or salad dressing
¼ cup French dressing
2 cups cut-up cooked chicken (about 12 ounces)
1 cup cherry tomatoes, cut into halves

Remove pea pods from package. Place pea pods in bowl of cool water until thawed; drain. Cook macaroni as directed on package—except add pea pods about 2 minutes before macaroni is done; drain. Rinse macaroni and pea pods with cold water; drain. Mix mayonnaise and French dressing in large bowl. Add macaroni mixture and remaining ingredients; toss.

**4 servings**

PER SERVING: Calories 510; Protein 31 g; Carbohydrate 36 g; Fat 27 g; Cholesterol 90 mg; Sodium 390 mg

## Chicken-Cucumber Salad

1 cup uncooked macaroni
¾ cup mayonnaise or salad dressing
1 tablespoon finely chopped onion
½ teaspoon salt
¼ teaspoon pepper
1½ cups cut-up cooked chicken
1 cup chopped cucumber

Cook macaroni as directed on package; drain. Rinse with cold water; drain. Mix mayonnaise, onion, salt and pepper. Toss with macaroni, chicken and cucumber. Cover and refrigerate about 2 hours or until chilled.     **4 servings**

PER SERVING: Calories 490; Protein 18 g; Carbohydrate 22 g; Fat 37 g; Cholesterol 45 mg; Sodium 550 mg

## Chicken and Tortellini Salad

1 package (8 ounces cheese-filled tortellini
1½ cups cut-up cooked chicken or turkey (about 8 ounces)
1 tablespoon chopped fresh or 1 teaspoon dried tarragon leaves
⅓ cup dry white wine or chicken broth
2 tablespoons olive or vegetable oil
2 tablespoons lemon juice
1 teaspoon sugar
½ teaspoon salt
¼ teaspoon pepper
3 cups bite-size pieces greens (spinach, leaf lettuce, romaine)
1 small red or green bell pepper, cut into ½-inch squares

Cook tortellini as directed on package; drain. Rinse with cold water; drain. Mix tortellini and chicken in large bowl.

Shake tarragon, wine, oil, lemon juice, sugar, salt and pepper in tightly covered container. Stir into tortellini mixture. Cover and refrigerate at least 2 hours. Toss tortellini mixture with greens and bell pepper just before serving.

**4 servings**

PER SERVING: Calories 270; Protein 15 g; Carbohydrate 31 g; Fat 8 g; Cholesterol 30 mg; Sodium 220 mg

## Baja Chicken-Pasta Salad

*Orzo is tiny pasta that resembles the shape of rice.*

1 cup uncooked orzo or ring macaroni
1 package (6 ounces) diced dried mixed fruit (about 1½ cups)
2 cups cut-up cooked chicken
1 cup cubed jicama
2 green onions (with tops), sliced
½ cup mayonnaise or salad dressing
2 tablespoons plain yogurt or sour cream
1 teaspoon ground red chilies
¼ teaspoon salt

Cook orzo as directed on package—except stir fruit into boiling water with orzo. Rinse orzo and fruit with cold water, drain.

Mix chicken, orzo, fruit, jicama and onions. Mix remaining ingredients; toss with chicken mixture. Cover and refrigerate about 2 hours or until chilled.            **6 servings**

PER  SERVING: Calories 455;  Protein 19 g;  Carbohydrate 63 g; Fat 16 g; Cholesterol 35 mg; Sodium 260 mg

---

## Varying Pasta

If you vary pasta shapes, be sure to substitute measure for measure, in similar sizes. For recipes that call for a specific amount of uncooked pasta, substitutions might be difficult because of variations in weight. Use the following pasta guide to figure out how much to prepare.

| Type | Uncooked | Cooked |
|---|---|---|
| Macaroni | 6 or 7 ounces | |
| | (2 cups) | 4 cups |
| Rotini | 8 ounces | 6 cups |
| Spaghetti | 7 or 8 ounces | 4 cups |
| Noodles | 8 ounces | 4 to 5 cups |

---

## Italian Pasta Salad

1 package (5 ounces) spiral macaroni
2 cups cooked cut-up chicken, beef or pork (about 12 ounces)
1 cup cherry tomato halves
1 cup broccoli flowerets
½ cup coarsely chopped unpared cucumber
½ cup thinly sliced carrot (about 1 medium)
½ cup reduced-calorie Italian dressing

Cook macaroni as directed on package; drain. Rinse with cold water, drain. Mix macaroni and remaining ingredients. Serve on salad greens if desired.            **4 servings**

PER  SERVING: Calories 260;  Protein 18 g;  Carbohydrate 34 g; Fat 6 g; Cholesterol 35 mg; Sodium 370 mg

## Macaroni-Chicken-Cantaloupe Salad

1 cup mayonnaise or salad dressing
1 tablespoon lemon juice
¼ teaspoon salt
¼ teaspoon pepper
2 cups cut-up cooked chicken
2 cups cooked macaroni or pasta
2 medium stalks celery, chopped (about 1 cup)
½ cup frozen green peas, thawed
½ cup cashew halves, if desired
1 medium cantaloupe, cut into 5 wedges

Mix mayonnaise, lemon juice, salt and pepper until blended. Toss with remaining ingredients. Cover and refrigerate about 2 hours or until chilled. Spoon salad onto cantaloupe wedges.            **5 servings**

PER  SERVING: Calories 680;  Protein 38 g;  Carbohydrate 35 g; Fat 43 g; Cholesterol 120 mg; Sodium 500 mg

## Turkey-Pasta Salad with Spinach Sauce

Spinach Sauce (right)
2 packages (5 ounces each) spiral
  macaroni
3 cups cut-up cooked turkey or chicken
½ cup sliced ripe olives
1 tablespoon olive or vegetable oil
1 teaspoon vinegar
1 tablespoon pine nuts or slivered
  almonds

Prepare Spinach Sauce. Cook macaroni as directed on package; drain. Rinse in cold water; drain. Toss macaroni and ½ cup of the Spinach Sauce. Mix turkey, olives, oil and vinegar. Spoon onto center of macaroni mixture. Sprinkle with pine nuts. Serve with remaining Spinach Sauce. **6 servings**

### Spinach Sauce

4 cups spinach leaves
1 cup fresh parsley sprigs
¼ cup lemon juice
3 large cloves garlic, cut into halves
½ cup grated Parmesan cheese
2 tablespoons olive or vegetable oil
1 tablespoon chopped fresh or 1 teaspoon dried basil leaves
½ teaspoon pepper

Place half each of the spinach, parsley, lemon juice and garlic in blender or food processor. Cover and blend on medium speed about 3 minutes, stopping blender frequently to scrape sides, or process, until spinach is finely chopped. Add remaining spinach, parsley, lemon juice and garlic; repeat. Add remaining ingredients. Cover and blend on medium speed about 2 minutes, stopping blender frequently to scrape sides, or process, until mixture is smooth.

PER SERVING: Calories 480; Protein 29 g; Carbohydrate 40 g; Fat 22 g; Cholesterol 65 mg; Sodium 300 mg

*Cajun Seafood and Noodles*

# 4

# Seafood and Pasta

## Cajun Seafood and Noodles

*If frozen shrimp and crab are not readily available, canned shrimp and crab are delicious.*

**6 ounces uncooked medium noodles (about 3 cups)**
**1 tablespoon vegetable oil**
**¾ cup chopped green bell pepper (about 1 medium)**
**½ cup chopped onion (about 1 medium)**
**2 tablespoons chopped fresh parsley**
**⅛ teaspoon ground red pepper (cayenne)**
**⅛ teaspoon pepper**
**2 cloves garlic, finely chopped**
**1 tablespoon all-purpose flour**
**1 can (16 ounces) whole tomatoes, undrained**
**1 package (10 ounces) frozen cut okra, thawed**
**1 package (6 ounces) frozen cooked small shrimp, thawed and drained**
**1 package (6 ounces) frozen crabmeat, thawed, drained and cartilage removed**

Cook noodles as directed on package; drain. Heat oil in 10-inch nonstick skillet over medium heat. Cook bell pepper, onion, parsley, red pepper, pepper and garlic 3 minutes, stirring frequently. Stir in flour and tomatoes; break up tomatoes.

Cook uncovered, stirring frequently, until mixture thickens and boils. Stir in okra, shrimp and crabmeat. Cook uncovered 5 minutes, stirring occasionally. Serve over noodles. **6 servings**

PER SERVING: Calories 225; Protein 15 g; Carbohydrate 31 g; Fat 5 g; Cholesterol 85 mg; Sodium 240 mg

## Pasta Amounts

When preparing pasta, allow ½ to ¾ cup cooked pasta per side or appetizer serving. If you plan to make pasta your main entrée, allow 1¼ to 1½ cups per serving. One ounce of dried pasta will yield approximately ½ cup of cooked pasta. This yield will vary slightly depending on the shape, type and size of pasta. And when you'd like a quick way to measure spaghetti, make a circle with your thumb and index finger about the size of a quarter, and fill it with pasta. You'll have 4 ounces of pasta, about 2 cups when cooked.

# Seafood Pasta with Vegetables

*Sea scallops, cut into ½-inch pieces, can be substituted for the bay scallops.*

½ cup chopped onion (about 1 medium)
2 cloves garlic, finely chopped
2 teaspoons vegetable oil
2 tablespoons cornstarch
1¾ cups clam- and tomato-flavored cocktail
½ pound bay scallops
1 pound frozen medium-size raw shrimp, thawed, peeled and deveined
2 cups ¼-inch slices yellow squash (about 2 small)
1 medium green bell pepper, cut into ¼-inch strips
2 tablespoons chopped fresh or 2 teaspoons dried basil leaves
1 teaspoon salt
¼ teaspoon pepper
6 ounces rotini or spiral macaroni, cooked and drained
1 cup 1-inch tomato pieces (about 1 medium)
2 tablespoons chopped fresh parsley

Cook and stir onion and garlic in oil in 4-quart nonstick Dutch oven over medium heat until onion is tender. Mix cornstarch and clam- and tomato-flavored cocktail; stir into onion mixture. Cook and stir until thickened and bubbly. Stir scallops, shrimp, squash, bell pepper, basil, salt and pepper into onion mixture. Cover and cook until seafood is done and vegetables are crisp-tender, about 5 minutes. Stir in rotini, tomato and parsley; heat through.          **8 servings**

PER SERVING: Calories 360; Protein 16 g; Carbohydrate 54 g; Fat 9 g; Cholesterol 195 mg; Sodium 1760 mg

# Spicy Scallops

*Can't find Anaheim chilies? Use a small red bell pepper. It will give the sauce a milder and sweeter flavor.*

1 red Anaheim chili, chopped
¼ cup sliced green onions with tops (about 3 medium)
2 tablespoons reduced-calorie margarine
2 tablespoons lime juice
2 pounds sea scallops
2 cups cubed fresh pineapple
1 cup Chinese pea pod halves (about 3 ounces)
3 cups hot cooked fettuccine

Cook chili, onions, margarine and lime juice in 10-inch skillet, stirring occasionally, until margarine is melted. Carefully stir in scallops. Cook over medium heat about 12 minutes, stirring frequently, until scallops are white. Stir in pineapple and pea pods. Heat until hot. Remove scallop mixture with slotted spoon; keep warm.

Heat liquid in skillet to boiling. Boil until slightly thickened and reduced to about half. Spoon scallop mixture onto fettuccine; pour liquid over scallop mixture.          **6 servings**

PER SERVING: Calories 335; Protein 39 g; Carbohydrate 34 g; Fat 6 g; Cholesterol 80 mg; Sodium 430 mg

## Scallops in Cream Sauce

1 pound scallops
1 green onion (with top), thinly sliced
¼ cup (½ stick) margarine or butter
¼ teaspoon salt
¼ cup dry white wine or chicken broth
2 teaspoons cornstarch
½ cup whipping (heavy) cream
4 cups hot cooked spinach noodles or fettuccine
½ cup finely shredded Swiss cheese

If scallops are large, cut into halves. Cook and stir onion in margarine in 10-inch skillet over medium-high heat until tender. Stir in scallops and salt. Cook, stirring frequently, until scallops are white, 3 to 4 minutes.

Mix wine and cornstarch; stir into scallop mixture. Heat to boiling, stirring constantly. Boil and stir 1 minute; reduce heat to medium. Stir in whipping cream. Heat until hot, 1 to 2 minutes. Toss noodles and cheese. Spoon scallop mixture over noodles. Serve with freshly ground pepper if desired. **6 servings**

PER SERVING: Calories 325; Protein 25 g; Carbohydrate 31 g; Fat 19 g; Cholesterol 90 mg; Sodium 420 mg

## Scampi with Fettuccine

1½ pounds fresh or frozen raw medium shrimp (in shells)
6 ounces uncooked spinach fettuccine
2 tablespoons olive or vegetable oil
2 tablespoons thinly sliced green onions (with tops)
1 tablespoon chopped fresh or 1½ teaspoons dried basil leaves
1 tablespoon chopped fresh parsley
2 tablespoons lemon juice
2 cloves garlic, finely chopped
¼ teaspoon salt

Peel shrimp. (If shrimp are frozen, do not thaw; peel in cold water.) Make a shallow cut lengthwise down back of each shrimp; wash out vein. Cook fettuccine as directed on package; drain.

Heat oil in 10-inch skillet, over medium heat. Stir in shrimp and remaining ingredients. Cook, stirring frequently, 2 to 3 minutes or until shrimp are pink; remove from heat. Toss fettuccine with shrimp mixture in skillet. **4 servings**

PER SERVING: Calories 335; Protein 24 g; Carbohydrate 32 g; Fat 12 g; Cholesterol 335 mg; Sodium 290 mg

## Shell Macaroni with Lobster

*This dish is wonderful with live lobsters, but you can also substitute frozen lobster tails. Use two frozen tails to equal 1 whole lobster.*

Sugo Sauce (page 11)
8 quarts water
2 tablespoons salt
2 tablespoons wine vinegar
2 live lobsters (about 1 pound each)
12 fresh sage leaves
1 package (32 ounces) large macaroni shells

Prepare Sugo Sauce; keep warm. Heat water, salt and vinegar to boiling in large kettle. Plunge lobsters headfirst into water. Cover and heat to boiling; reduce heat. Simmer uncovered 10 to 12 minutes or until lobsters are bright red. Drain and cool slightly.

Place each lobster on its back; cut lengthwise in half. Remove the stomach, which is just behind the head, and the intestinal vein, which runs from the stomach to the tip of the tail. Do not discard the green liver and coral roe. Remove meat. Crack claws, remove meat. Stir lobster meat, liver, roe and sage leaves into Sugo Sauce. Heat to boiling; reduce heat. Simmer uncovered 10 minutes, stirring occasionally.

Cook macaroni as directed on package; drain. Pour sauce over macaroni.          **6 servings**

PER SERVING: Calories 700; Protein 30 g; Carbohydrate 132 g; Fat 6 g; Cholesterol 25 mg; Sodium 1100 mg

## Angel Hair Pasta with Shrimp

1 package (16 ounces) capellini (angel hair pasta)
¼ cup olive oil
2 tablespoons chopped fresh parsley
2 cloves garlic, finely chopped
1 small red chili, seeded and finely chopped
⅓ cup dry white wine or chicken broth
½ teaspoon freshly grated nutmeg
12 ounces frozen peeled raw small shrimp, thawed

Cook capellini as directed on package. Meanwhile, heat oil in 4-quart Dutch oven or 12-inch skillet over medium-high heat. Sauté parsley, garlic and chili in oil. Stir in wine, nutmeg and shrimp; reduce heat. Cover and simmer about 5 minutes or until shrimp are pink.

Drain capellini; mix with shrimp mixture in Dutch oven. Cook over medium heat 2 minutes, stirring occasionally.          **4 servings**

PER SERVING: Calories 585; Protein 27 g; Carbohydrate 76 g; Fat 19 g; Cholesterol 220 mg; Sodium 160 mg

**Angel Hair Pasta with Shrimp**

## Spaghetti with Mussel Sauce

2 pounds fresh mussels
2 tablespoons olive oil
2 tablespoons chopped fresh parsley
2 cloves garlic, finely chopped
2 cans (28 ounces each) Italian pear-
    shaped tomatoes, drained and chopped
1 medium red bell pepper, chopped
1 package (16 ounces) spaghetti
1 tablespoon grated Parmesan cheese
Freshly ground pepper

Discard any broken-shell or open (dead) mussels. Wash remaining mussels, removing any barnacles with a dull paring knife. Remove beards by tugging them away from shells.

Heat oil in 10-inch skillet over medium-high heat. Sauté parsley and garlic in oil. Stir in tomatoes and bell pepper. Cook 5 minutes, stirring frequently, until pepper is tender.

Add mussels; cover and cook about 5 minutes or until mussels open. Discard unopened mussels. Remove mussels from shells and discard shells. Stir mussels into sauce.

Cook spaghetti as directed on package; drain. Mix spaghetti and sauce; top with cheese. Serve with pepper. **6 servings**

PER SERVING: Calories 435; Protein 19 g; Carbohydrate 74 g; Fat 7 g; Cholesterol 15 mg; Sodium 580 mg

## Tuna-Macaroni Skillet

*A hot and hearty recipe in short order.*

1 can (10¾ ounces) condensed cream of
    chicken soup
2¼ cups water
1 package (10 ounces) frozen mixed
    vegetables
1 package (7 ounces) elbow macaroni
¼ teaspoon dried dill weed
2 cans (6½ ounces each) tuna, drained
1 can (2.8 ounces) French fried onions

Mix soup and water in 10-inch skillet; stir in vegetables, macaroni and dill weed. Heat to boiling, stirring occasionally; reduce heat. Cover and simmer, stirring occasionally, until macaroni is tender, about 15 minutes. Stir in tuna; heat until hot, about 3 minutes. Sprinkle with onions.

**6 servings**

PER SERVING: Calories 355; Protein 24 g; Carbohydrate 40 g; Fat 11 g; Cholesterol 15 mg; Sodium 700 mg

# Dried and Fresh Pasta

Pasta is available in two forms: dried and fresh. Dried pasta is the most common form and is usually found prepackaged or in serve-yourself bulk form. Fresh pasta can be found in the refrigerated section of the supermarket. Dried pasta can be stored indefinitely, but fresh pasta is perishable and should be covered and refrigerated. If you buy prepackaged fresh pasta, leave it in the original packaging. Fresh pasta cooks faster than dried pasta, so keep this simple rule in mind: the fresher the pasta, the shorter the cooking time.

## Tuna Noodles Romanoff

4 cups uncooked egg noodles (about 8 ounces)
2 cans (6½ ounces each) tuna, drained
1 jar (2 ounces) diced pimientos, drained
1 cup sliced mushrooms
1½ cups sour cream
¾ cup milk
1 tablespoon chopped fresh chives
1 teaspoon salt
¼ teaspoon pepper
¼ cup dry bread crumbs
¼ cup grated Romano cheese
2 tablespoons margarine or butter, melted

Heat oven to 350°. Cook noodles as directed on package; drain. Mix noodles, tuna, pimientos, mushrooms, sour cream, milk, chives, salt and pepper in ungreased 2-quart casserole or square baking dish, 8 × 8 × 2 inches. Mix bread crumbs, cheese and margarine; sprinkle over tuna mixture. Bake uncovered 35 to 40 minutes or until hot and bubbly.

**6 to 8 servings**

TO SERVE LATER: Prepare casserole. Cover and refrigerate up to 24 hours. Bake covered in 350° oven 40 minutes. Uncover and bake 10 minutes longer.

PER SERVING: Calories 415; Protein 24 g; Carbohydrate 35 g; Fat 20 g; Cholesterol 95 mg; Sodium 980 mg

## Tuna-Asparagus Casserole

*This is a good dish to make ahead and serve the next day.*

1 package (10 ounces) frozen cut asparagus, cooked and drained
1 can (10¾ ounces) condensed cream of chicken soup
1 can (4 ounces) mushroom stems and pieces, undrained
½ cup sour cream
1 can (6½ ounces) tuna, drained
1 small green bell pepper, chopped (about ½ cup)
¼ cup slivered almonds
2 tablespoons chopped pimiento
2½ cups uncooked egg noodles (about 5 ounces)
1 cup shredded Cheddar cheese (4 ounces)

Heat oven to 350°. Arrange asparagus in ungreased 2-quart casserole or square baking dish, 8 × 8 × 2 inches. Mix soup, mushrooms and sour cream in medium bowl. Stir in tuna, bell pepper, almonds and pimiento. Fold in noodles. Spread over asparagus.

Cover and bake 35 to 40 minutes or until noodles are tender. Sprinkle with cheese. Bake uncovered 5 minutes longer. **6 servings**

TO SERVE LATER: Prepare casserole. Cover and refrigerate up to 24 hours. Bake covered in 350° oven 50 to 55 minutes or until noodles are tender. Sprinkle with cheese. Bake uncovered 5 minutes longer.

PER SERVING: Calories 340; Protein 20 g; Carbohydrate 27 g; Fat 18 g; Cholesterol 70 mg; Sodium 750 mg

## Salmon and Macaroni

*Salmon makes an interesting change from tuna in this casserole.*

1 medium onion, chopped (about ½ cup)
¼ cup (½ stick) margarine or butter
2 tablespoons all-purpose flour
1 can (15½ ounces) salmon, drained and liquid reserved
1¾ cups milk
¼ teaspoon salt
⅛ teaspoon paprika
1 tablespoon lemon juice
¼ cup chopped fresh parsley
3 cups hot, cooked elbow macaroni
1 cup shredded Cheddar cheese (4 ounces)

Heat oven to 375°. Cook onion in margarine, stirring frequently, until tender. Stir in flour until blended. Cook over low heat, stirring constantly, until smooth and bubbly; remove from heat. Stir in reserved salmon liquid and the milk. Cook over low heat, stirring constantly, until slightly thickened; remove from heat. Stir in salt, paprika, lemon juice and parsley.

Layer macaroni, salmon and ¾ cup of the cheese in ungreased 2-quart casserole. Pour sauce over cheese. Sprinkle with remaining cheese. Bake uncovered 20 to 25 minutes or until cheese is brown. **6 to 8 servings**

TO SERVE LATER: Prepare casserole. Cover and refrigerate up to 24 hours. Bake covered in 350° oven 30 minutes. Uncover and bake 10 minutes longer or until cheese is brown.

PER SERVING: Calories 380; Protein 25 g; Carbohydrate 21 g; Fat 21 g; Cholesterol 45 mg; Sodium 590 mg

## Seafood Lasagne

½ cup (1 stick) margarine or butter
2 cloves garlic, crushed
½ cup all-purpose flour
½ teaspoon salt
2 cups milk
2 cups chicken broth
2 cups shredded mozzarella cheese (8 ounces)
½ cup sliced green onions (with tops)
1 tablespoon chopped fresh or 1 teaspoon dried basil leaves
¼ teaspoon pepper
8 ounces uncooked lasagne noodles (9 or 10 noodles)
1 cup small curd creamed cottage cheese
1 cup cooked crabmeat or ½-inch pieces seafood sticks
1 cup bite-size pieces of cooked shrimp
½ cup grated Parmesan cheese

Heat oven to 350°. Heat margarine in 3-quart saucepan over low heat until melted. Add garlic. Stir in flour and salt. Cook, stirring constantly, until bubbly; remove from heat. Stir in milk and broth. Heat to boiling, stirring constantly. Boil and stir 1 minute. Stir in mozzarella cheese, onions, basil and pepper. Cook over low heat, stirring constantly, until cheese is melted.

Spread one-fourth of the cheese sauce (about 1½ cups) in ungreased rectangular baking dish, 13 × 9 × 2 inches. Top with 3 or 4 uncooked noodles, overlapping if necessary. Spread cottage cheese over noodles in dish. Repeat with one-fourth of the cheese sauce and 3 or 4 noodles. Top with crabmeat, shrimp and one-fourth of the cheese sauce. Top with remaining noodles and cheese sauce. Sprinkle with Parmesan cheese.

Bake uncovered 35 to 40 minutes or until noodles are tender. Let stand 15 minutes before cutting. **12 servings**

PER SERVING: Calories 285; Protein 16 g; Carbohydrate 19 g; Fat 16 g; Cholesterol 60 mg; Sodium 650 mg

## Seafood-stuffed Shells

15 uncooked jumbo macaroni shells
2 cups small curd creamed cottage
    cheese
1/4 cup plus 2 tablespoons milk
1 tablespoon lemon juice
1 teaspoon salt
1/8 teaspoon pepper
1/2 cup parsley sprigs
1 1/2 teaspoons chopped fresh or 1/2 tea-
    spoon dried basil leaves
2 cloves garlic, crushed
2 medium stalks celery, sliced (about 1
    cup)
1 medium zucchini, coarsely shredded
1 medium onion, chopped (about 1/2 cup)
6 seafood legs, cut into 1/2-inch pieces
2 cans (4 1/2 ounces each) large shrimp,
    rinsed and drained
Salad greens

Prepare macaroni shells as directed on package; drain. Refrigerate at least 1 hour.

Place cottage cheese, milk, lemon juice, salt and
pepper in blender container. Cover and blend
on high speed, stopping blender occasionally to
scrape sides, until smooth, about 2 minutes. Remove 1/2 cup; reserve. Add parsley, basil and
garlic to remaining mixture in blender container.
Cover and blend on high speed until smooth,
about 45 seconds; refrigerate.

Mix celery, zucchini, onion, seafood legs, shrimp
and reserved 1/2 cup cottage cheese mixture.
Spoon into macaroni shells. Refrigerate at least
1 hour.

Place stuffed shells on salad greens; serve parsley mixture with shells. (If parsley mixture is too
thick, stir in additional milk until of desired
consistency.)                    **5 servings**

PER  SERVING: Calories 430;  Protein 37 g;  Carbohydrate 55 g; Fat 7 g; Cholesterol 110 mg; Sodium 2270 mg

## Tuna Toss

2 cans (6 1/2 ounces each) tuna in water,
    drained
2 medium tomatoes, chopped (about 1 1/2
    cups)
2 cloves garlic, crushed
1 small onion, thinly sliced and sepa-
    rated into rings
1/2 cup pitted small ripe olives
2 tablespoons chopped fresh parsley
2 tablespoons olive or vegetable oil
1/2 teaspoon salt
1 1/2 teaspoons chopped fresh or 1/2 tea-
    spoon dried basil leaves
3/4 teaspoon chopped fresh or 1/4 tea-
    spoon dried oregano leaves
1/8 teaspoon coarsely ground pepper
2 cups uncooked bow-tie pasta (farfalle)

Mix all ingredients except bow-tie pasta. Cover
and refrigerate at least 2 hours but no longer
than 24 hours.

Cook pasta as directed on package; drain. Immediately toss with tuna mixture. Serve salad
on lettuce leaves and garnish with anchovies, if
desired.                    **5 servings**

PER  SERVING: Calories 375;  Protein 27 g;  Carbohydrate 46 g; Fat 9 g; Cholesterol 10 mg; Sodium 580 mg

**Dilled Pasta Salad with Smoked Fish**

## Dilled Pasta Salad with Smoked Fish

*A simple, satisfying salad for a hot day.*

2 cups uncooked rotini or spiral
    macaroni
½ cup mayonnaise or salad dressing
¼ cup plain yogurt or sour cream
1 tablespoon chopped fresh or ½ tea-
    spoon dried dill weed
½ teaspoon dry mustard
¼ teaspoon salt
¼ teaspoon pepper
1 can (2¼ ounces) sliced pitted ripe ol-
    ives, drained (about ½ cup)
2 green onions (with tops), thinly sliced
1 medium zucchini, thinly sliced (about 2
    cups)
1 medium carrot, thinly sliced (about ½
    cup)
2 cups flaked boneless smoked whitefish
    or salmon (about ⅔ pound)

Cook rotini as directed on package; drain. Rinse pasta in cold water; drain. Mix mayonnaise, yogurt, dill weed, mustard, salt and pepper in large bowl. Add rotini and remaining ingredients except smoked fish; toss. Gently stir in smoked fish. **4 servings**

PER SERVING: Calories 580; Protein 30 g; Carbohydrate 57 g; Fat 26 g; Cholesterol 75 mg; Sodium 1040 mg

## Macaroni-Shrimp Salad

1½ cups uncooked elbow or spiral maca-
    roni (about 6 ounces)
1 package (10 ounces) frozen green peas
1 cup shredded Cheddar cheese (4
    ounces)
¾ cup mayonnaise or salad dressing
8 green onions (with tops), sliced (about
    ½ cup)
⅓ cup sweet pickle relish
1 stalk celery, sliced (about ½ cup)
1 can (4½ ounces) tiny shrimp, rinsed
    and drained
½ head iceberg lettuce, torn into bite-size
    pieces (about 3 cups)
6 slices bacon, crisply cooked and
    crumbled

Cook macaroni as directed on package. Rinse in cold water and drain. Rinse frozen peas with cold water to separate; drain. Mix macaroni, peas and remaining ingredients except lettuce and bacon. Cover and refrigerate about 4 hours or until chilled.

Just before serving, mix macaroni mixture, lettuce and bacon. **6 servings**

PER SERVING: Calories 480; Protein 15 g; Carbohydrate 35 g; Fat 31 g; Cholesterol 40 mg; Sodium 490 mg

# Seafood-Pasta Salad

*Cilantro and ginger add cooling flavors to this enticing salad.*

Ginger Dressing (below)
8 ounces uncooked vermicelli
2 cups bite-size pieces cooked seafood or 1 package (8 ounces) frozen salad-style imitation crabmeat, thawed
½ cup coarsely chopped jicama or water chestnuts
¼ cup chopped fresh cilantro or parsley
2 medium carrots, shredded (about 1¼ cups)
1 medium cucumber, coarsely chopped (about 1 cup)

Prepare Ginger Dressing. Break vermicelli in half. Cook as directed on package; drain. Rinse with cold water; drain. Toss vermicelli, seafood, jicama, cilantro, carrots and cucumber with Ginger Dressing. Spoon onto salad greens if desired. **6 servings**

PER SERVING: Calories 295; Protein 13 g; Carbohydrate 35 g; Fat 11 g; Cholesterol 50 mg; Sodium 360 mg

## Ginger Dressing

⅓ cup mayonnaise or salad dressing
½ cup plain yogurt
1 tablespoon soy sauce
1 teaspoon sugar
½ teaspoon ground ginger
Dash of red pepper sauce, hot chili oil or hot sesame oil

Mix all ingredients.

# Tarragon-Seafood Salad

3 cups uncooked bow-tie macaroni (farfalle) (about 6 ounces)
4 ounces pea pods, cut into halves
2 tablespoons olive or vegetable oil
1 tablespoon chopped fresh or 1 teaspoon dried tarragon leaves
½ teaspoon salt
¼ teaspoon white pepper
2 cloves garlic, finely chopped
¾ pound seafood sticks, cut into ½-inch pieces

Cook pasta as directed on package—except add pea pods 1 minute before pasta is done; drain. Rinse pasta and pea pods in cold water; drain. Gently toss all ingredients. **4 servings**

PER SERVING: Calories 520; Protein 26 g; Carbohydrate 84 g; Fat 9 g; Cholesterol 25 mg; Sodium 1010 mg

**Tarragon-Seafood Salad**

*Quick Lasagne*

# 5

# Meat and Pasta

## Quick Lasagne

*Just the recipe when you're short on time.*

½ **pound ground beef**
1 **medium clove garlic, chopped**
1 **teaspoon Italian seasoning**
1 **cup spaghetti sauce**
6 **uncooked instant lasagne noodles**
   **(each about 6½ × 3 inches)**
1 **container (12 ounces) low-fat cottage**
   **cheese**
1 **cup shredded Monterey Jack cheese (4**
   **ounces)**
2 **tablespoons grated Parmesan cheese**

Heat oven to 400°. Cook ground beef and garlic in 10-inch skillet over medium heat, stirring frequently, until ground beef is brown; drain. Stir in Italian seasoning and spaghetti sauce. Heat to boiling; remove from heat.

Spread ¼ cup beef mixture in square pan, 8 × 8 × 2 or 9 × 9 × 2 inches. Top with 2 lasagne noodles. Spread one-third of the beef mixture (about ½ cup) over noodles in pan. Spread one-third of the cottage cheese (about ½ cup) over beef mixture.

Sprinkle with one-third of the Monterey Jack cheese (about ⅓ cup) on top. Repeat layering twice. Sprinkle with Parmesan cheese. Bake about 10 minutes or until hot and cheese is melted. Let stand 5 minutes before serving.

**4 servings**

PER SERVING: Calories 465; Protein 34 g; Carbohydrate 33 g; Fat 22 g; Cholesterol 70 mg; Sodium 1000 mg

## Tomatoes

Tomatoes were introduced to Europe after they were discovered in America, but they were used only as ornamental plants. Neapolitans were the first to use tomatoes as a food source, during a famine in the seventeenth century. The region around Naples is still where wonderful pear-shaped tomatoes are grown and canned. They make excellent sauces, having more pulp, more sweetness and lower acidity than other tomatoes.

## Lasagne

1 pound ground beef
2 cloves garlic, minced
3 cans (8 ounces each) tomato sauce*
½ teaspoon salt
¼ teaspoon pepper
½ teaspoon diced oregano leaves
1 package (8 ounces) uncooked lasagne noodles
1 carton (12 ounces) creamed cottage cheese (1½ cups)
2 cups shredded mozzarella or Swiss cheese (8 ounces)
⅓ cup grated Parmesan cheese

Cook and stir meat and garlic in large skillet until meat is brown. Drain off fat. Stir in tomato sauce, salt, pepper and oregano leaves. Cover and simmer 20 minutes.

While meat sauce is simmering, cook noodles as directed on package; drain.

Heat oven to 350°. In ungreased baking pan, 13 × 9 × 2 inches, or baking dish, 11¾ × 7½ × 1¾ inches, layer half each of the noodles, meat sauce, cottage cheese and mozzarella cheese; repeat. Sprinkle Parmesan cheese over top. Bake uncovered until hot and bubbly, about 40 minutes. **6 servings**

PER SERVING: Calories 520; Protein 40 g; Carbohydrate 41 g; Fat 22 g; Cholesterol 75 mg; Sodium 1410 mg

*You can substitute 1 can (16 ounces) tomatoes and 1 can (6 ounces) tomato paste for the tomato sauce.

## Lasagne Roll-ups

*With its unusual shape, this lasagne is easy to serve, and perfect for buffets.*

6 uncooked lasagne noodles
6 uncooked spinach lasagne noodles
1 pound ground beef
1 large onion, chopped (about 1 cup)
1 jar (15½ ounces) spaghetti sauce
1 can (8 ounces) mushroom stems and pieces, undrained
1 carton (15 ounces) ricotta cheese or creamed cottage cheese (about 2 cups)
1 package (10 ounces) frozen chopped spinach, thawed and well drained
1 cup shredded mozzarella cheese (4 ounces)
¼ cup grated Parmesan cheese
1 teaspoon salt
¼ teaspoon pepper
2 cloves garlic, crushed

Heat oven to 350°. Cook noodles as directed on package; drain. Cover noodles with cold water. Cook ground beef and onion in 10-inch skillet, stirring occasionally, until beef is light brown; drain. Stir in spaghetti sauce and mushrooms. Heat to boiling. Pour into rectangular baking dish, 11 × 7 × 1½ inches.

Mix remaining ingredients. Drain noodles. Spread 3 tablespoons of the cheese mixture to edges of 1 noodle. Roll up; cut roll in half. Place cut sides down in beef mixture. Repeat with remaining noodles. Cover and bake about 30 minutes or until hot and bubbly. Serve with grated Parmesan cheese if desired. **8 servings**

PER SERVING: Calories 525; Protein 33 g; Carbohydrate 49 g; Fat 24 g; Cholesterol 135 mg; Sodium 1150 mg

## Green Lasagne with Two Sauces

**Meat Sauce (below)**
**Cheese Filling (right)**
**Creamy Sauce (right)**
**12 spinach lasagne noodles, cooked and drained**

Heat oven to 350°. Prepare Meat Sauce, Cheese Filling and Creamy Sauce. Reserve ½ cup of the Cheese Filling. Spread 1 cup of the Meat Sauce in ungreased oblong baking dish, 13½ × 9 × 2 inches. Layer 3 lasagne noodles, half of the Creamy Sauce, half of the remaining Cheese Filling, 3 lasagne noodles and half of the remaining Meat Sauce; repeat. Sprinkle with reserved Cheese Filling. Cook uncovered in oven until hot and bubbly, about 35 minutes. Let stand 10 minutes before cutting.

**12 servings**

PER SERVING: Calories 345; Protein 20 g; Carbohydrate 24 g; Fat 19 g; Cholesterol 60 mg; Sodium 850 mg

### Meat Sauce

**8 ounces bulk Italian sausage, crumbled**
**4 ounces smoked sliced chicken or turkey, finely chopped**
**1 large onion, finely chopped (about 1 cup)**
**1 medium stalk celery, finely chopped**
**1 medium carrot, finely shredded**
**2 cloves garlic, finely chopped**
**1¾ cups water**
**¾ cup dry red wine or beef broth**
**⅓ cup tomato paste**
**½ teaspoon Italian seasoning**
**⅛ teaspoon pepper**
**Dash of ground nutmeg**

Cook and stir sausage until light brown; drain. Stir in remaining ingredients. Heat to boiling; reduce heat. Simmer uncovered, stirring occasionally, 1 hour.

### Cheese Filling

**2 cups shredded mozzarella cheese**
**1½ cups grated Parmesan cheese**
**¼ cup chopped parsley**

Toss cheeses and parsley.

### Creamy Sauce

**⅓ cup margarine or butter**
**⅓ cup all-purpose flour**
**1 teaspoon salt**
**Dash of ground nutmeg**
**3 cups milk**

Heat margarine over low heat until melted. Blend in flour, salt and nutmeg. Cook over low heat, stirring constantly, until smooth and bubbly; remove from heat. Stir in milk. Heat to boiling, stirring constantly. Boil and stir 1 minute; cover and keep warm. (If sauce thickens, beat in small amount of milk. Sauce should be the consistency of heavy cream.)

## Manicotti

*This is nice served with garlic bread and a tossed green salad.*

  1 pound ground beef
  ¼ cup chopped onion (about 1 small)
  3 slices bread, torn into small pieces
  1½ cups shredded mozzarella cheese
  1 egg
  ½ cup milk
  1 tablespoon chopped fresh parsley
  ¼ teaspoon pepper
  1 package (8 ounces) uncooked manicotti shells
  1 can (4 ounces) mushroom stems and pieces, undrained
  1 can (15 ounces) tomato sauce
  1 can (12 ounces) tomato paste
  ¼ cup chopped onion (about 1 small)
  1 clove garlic, minced
  4 cups water
  1 tablespoon Italian seasoning
  ½ teaspoon sugar
  ½ teaspoon salt
  ⅛ teaspoon pepper
  ⅓ cup grated Parmesan cheese

Cook and stir meat and ¼ cup onion in large skillet until meat is brown. Drain off fat. Remove from heat; stir in bread, mozzarella, egg, milk, parsley, and pepper.

Fill uncooked manicotti shells, packing the filling into both ends. Place shells in ungreased baking pan, 13 × 9 × 2 inches.

Heat oven to 375°. Heat mushrooms (with liquid) and remaining ingredients except cheese to boiling, stirring occasionally. Reduce heat and simmer uncovered 5 minutes. Pour sauce over shells. Cover with aluminum foil and bake until shells are tender, 1½ to 1¾ hours. Sprinkle with cheese. Cool 5 to 10 minutes before serving. **6 servings**

PER SERVING: Calories 545; Protein 35 g; Carbohydrate 56 g; Fat 20 g; Cholesterol 100 mg; Sodium 1490 mg

## Baked Macaroni with Beef and Cheese

  7 ounces uncooked ziti or elbow macaroni (about 2 cups)
  ¾ pound ground beef
  1 small onion, chopped (about ¼ cup)
  1 can (15 ounces) tomato sauce
  1 teaspoon salt
  1½ cups grated Parmesan or Romano cheese (6 ounces)
  ⅛ teaspoon ground cinnamon
  1¼ cups milk
  3 tablespoons margarine or butter
  2 eggs, beaten
  ⅛ teaspoon ground nutmeg

Heat oven to 325°. Cook macaroni as directed on package; drain. Cook and stir beef and onion in 10-inch skillet until beef is light brown; drain. Stir in tomato sauce and salt. Spread half the macaroni in greased square baking dish, 8 × 8 × 2 inches; cover with beef mixture. Mix ½ cup of the cheese and the cinnamon; sprinkle over beef mixture. Cover with remaining macaroni.

Cook and stir milk and margarine in 2-quart saucepan until margarine is melted. Remove from heat. Stir at least half the milk mixture gradually into beaten eggs. Blend into milk mixture in saucepan; pour over macaroni. Sprinkle with remaining 1 cup cheese. Cook uncovered in oven until brown and center is set, about 50 minutes. Sprinkle with nutmeg. Garnish with parsley, if desired. **6 servings**

PER SERVING Calories 500; Protein 31 g; Carbohydrate 35 g; Fat 26 g; Cholesterol 130 mg; Sodium 1450 mg

## Easy Beef Casserole

*This recipe is extra easy because you don't cook the macaroni before assembling the casserole.*

1½ cups cut-up cooked beef
1½ cups uncooked elbow macaroni
  (about 5 ounces)
½ cup milk
1½ teaspoons dried basil leaves
½ teaspoon garlic powder
⅛ teaspoon pepper
2 medium stalks celery, sliced (about 1 cup)
1 small onion, chopped (about ¼ cup)
1 jar (8 ounces) mushroom stems and pieces, undrained
1 can (8 ounces) tomato sauce

Heat oven to 350°. Mix all ingredients in ungreased 2-quart casserole. Cover and bake 30 minutes; stir. Cover and bake about 20 minutes longer or until macaroni is tender.

**6 servings**

PER SERVING: Calories 185; Protein 15 g; Carbohydrate 24 g; Fat 3 g; Cholesterol 35 mg; Sodium 260 mg

## Skillet Beef and Noodles

1 pound ground beef
1 envelope (about 1½ ounces) onion soup mix
1 can (1 pound 12 ounces) tomatoes
4 ounces uncooked noodles (about 2 cups)

In large skillet, cook and stir ground beef until brown. Stir in remaining ingredients; heat to boiling. Reduce heat; cover and simmer until noodles are tender, about 20 minutes, stirring occasionally. **4 servings**

PER SERVING: Calories 400; Protein 27 g; Carbohydrate 32 g; Fat 18 g; Cholesterol 90 mg; Sodium 1250 mg

## Pasta with Chunky Tomato Sauce

1 pound lean ground beef
1 large onion, chopped (about 1 cup)
1 clove garlic, crushed
1 tablespoon chopped fresh or 1 teaspoon dried oregano leaves
2 teaspoons chopped fresh or ¾ teaspoon dried basil leaves
1½ teaspoons chopped fresh or ½ teaspoon dried marjoram leaves
1 teaspoon sugar
¾ teaspoon salt
1 can (16 ounces) whole tomatoes, undrained
1 can (8 ounces) tomato sauce
5 cups hot cooked pasta or spaghetti
Grated Parmesan cheese

Cook ground beef, onion and garlic in 10-inch skillet, stirring occasionally, until beef is brown; drain. Stir in remaining ingredients except pasta and cheese; break up tomatoes. Heat to boiling; reduce heat. Cover and simmer about 1 hour, stirring occasionally. Serve over pasta. Sprinkle with cheese. **6 servings**

PER SERVING: Calories 310; Protein 27 g; Carbohydrate 37 g; Fat 6 g; Cholesterol 60 mg; Sodium 740 mg

## Ground Beef in Red Wine Sauce

*Lean ground beef trims calories but leaves all the robust flavor.*

1½ pounds lean ground beef
1 medium onion, finely chopped (about ½ cup)
2 cloves garlic, finely chopped
¼ cup olive or vegetable oil
1 small green bell pepper, chopped (about ½ cup)
¼ cup chopped fresh parsley
1 tablespoon chopped fresh or ¾ teaspoon dried basil leaves
2 teaspoons chopped fresh or ½ teaspoon dried oregano leaves
1 teaspoon salt
½ teaspoon pepper
¼ teaspoon sugar
3 cans (8 ounces each) tomato sauce
1 can (4 ounces) mushroom stems and pieces, undrained
1 cup dry red wine or beef broth
10 cups hot cooked fettuccine

Cook ground beef, onion and garlic in oil in Dutch oven, stirring occasionally, until beef is brown; drain. Stir in remaining ingredients except wine and fettuccine. Heat to boiling; reduce heat. Cover and simmer 1 hour, stirring occasionally.

Stir in wine. Cover and simmer 30 minutes, stirring occasionally. Uncover and simmer 30 minutes longer, stirring occasionally. Serve over hot fettuccine. **12 servings**

PER SERVING: Calories 295; Protein 19 g; Carbohydrate 33 g; Fat 8 g; Cholesterol 40 mg; Sodium 530 mg

## Spaghetti and Meatballs

*An all-time favorite!*

1 tablespoon chopped fresh or 1 teaspoon dried oregano leaves
1 tablespoon chopped fresh or 1 teaspoon dried basil leaves
2 teaspoons chopped fresh or ½ teaspoon dried marjoram leaves
1 teaspoon sugar
½ teaspoon salt
1 large onion, chopped (about 1 cup)
1 clove garlic, crushed
1 can (16 ounces) whole tomatoes, undrained
1 can (8 ounces) tomato sauce
Meatballs (right)
4 cups hot cooked spaghetti

Mix all ingredients except Meatballs and spaghetti in 3-quart saucepan; break up tomatoes. Heat to boiling; reduce heat. Cover and simmer 30 minutes, stirring occasionally.

Prepare Meatballs; drain. Stir meatballs into tomato mixture. Cover and simmer 30 minutes longer, stirring occasionally. Serve over spaghetti and, if desired, with grated Parmesan cheese. **6 servings**

PER SERVING: Calories 385; Protein 23 g; Carbohydrate 39 g; Fat 15 g; Cholesterol 90 mg; Sodium 810 mg

## Meatballs

1 pound ground beef
½ cup dry bread crumbs
¼ cup milk
½ teaspoon salt
½ teaspoon Worcestershire sauce
¼ teaspoon pepper
1 small onion, chopped (about ¼ cup)
1 egg

Heat oven to 400°. Mix all ingredients. Shape into twenty 1½-inch meatballs. Place in rectangular pan, 13 × 9 × 2 inches. Bake 20 to 25 minutes or until no longer pink inside.

# Meatballs in Dijon Sauce

*A Dijon mustard sauce adds excitement to these sophisticated meatballs.*

1 pound lean ground beef
1 slice whole wheat bread, crumbled
¼ cup finely chopped onion (about 1 small)
1 tablespoon Dijon mustard
¼ teaspoon salt
¼ teaspoon pepper
Dijon Sauce ( right )
3 cups hot cooked noodles

Heat oven to 400°. Mix all ingredients except Dijon Sauce and noodles; shape into twenty-four 1¼-inch meatballs. Place on rack sprayed with nonstick cooking spray in broiler pan. Bake uncovered until done and light brown, 20 to 25 minutes.

Prepare Dijon Sauce; add meatballs, stirring gently, until meatballs are hot. Serve over noodles.                    **6 servings**

## Dijon Sauce

3 tablespoons all-purpose flour
1 tablespoon cornstarch
1½ teaspoons instant beef bouillon
1 cup water
1 cup skim milk
3 tablespoons finely chopped chives
2 tablespoons Dijon mustard
¼ teaspoon pepper
1 teaspoon lemon juice

Mix flour, cornstarch, bouillon (dry) and water in 2-quart saucepan; stir in remaining ingredients. Cook over medium heat until mixture thickens and boils, stirring constantly. Boil and stir 1 minute.

PER SERVING: Calories 310; Protein 20 g; Carbohydrate 26 g; Fat 14 g; Cholesterol 55 mg; Sodium 400 mg

**Sauerbraten Meatballs and Noodles**

## Sauerbraten Meatballs and Noodles

1 pound lean ground beef or pork
⅓ cup crushed gingersnaps (about 6 gingersnaps)
½ cup finely chopped onion (about 1 medium)
¼ cup water
½ teaspoon salt
¼ teaspoon pepper
6 ounces uncooked egg noodles or spaetzle (about 3 cups)
1 cup beef broth
¼ cup apple cider vinegar
1 tablespoon sugar
¼ cup crushed gingersnaps (about 4 gingersnaps)
2 tablespoons raisins

Heat oven to 400°. Mix ground beef, ⅓ cup gingersnaps, the onion, water, salt and pepper. Shape mixture into 24 meatballs. Spray rack in broiler pan with nonstick cooking spray. Place meatballs on rack. Bake uncovered 20 to 25 minutes or until done and light brown.

Cook noodles as directed on package; drain. Mix remaining ingredients except raisins in 1½-quart saucepan. Cook over medium heat, stirring constantly, until mixture thickens and boils. Stir in raisins and meatballs. Heat until hot. Serve over noodles.　　　　　　　　　　**6 servings**

PER SERVING: Calories 300; Protein 24 g; Carbohydrate 34 g; Fat 7 g; Cholesterol 85 mg; Sodium 480 mg

## One-Skillet Spaghetti

*Cook this spaghetti on the stove or in the oven, whichever suits you best.*

1 pound ground beef
2 medium onions, chopped (about 1 cup)
1 can (29 ounces) tomatoes, undrained
¾ cup chopped green bell pepper
½ cup water
1 can (4 ounces) mushroom stems and pieces, drained
2 teaspoons salt
1 teaspoon sugar
1 teaspoon chili powder
1 package (7 ounces) uncooked thin spaghetti, broken into pieces
1 cup shredded Cheddar cheese (4 ounces)

Cook and stir meat and onions in large skillet or Dutch oven until meat is brown. Drain off fat. Stir in tomatoes (with liquid) and remaining ingredients except Cheddar cheese; break up tomatoes.　　　　　　　　　　**7 servings**

PER SERVING: Calories 355; Protein 21 g; Carbohydrate 32 g; Fat 16 g; Cholesterol 55 mg; Sodium 1010 mg

TO COOK IN SKILLET: Heat mixture to boiling. Reduce heat; cover and simmer, stirring occasionally, until spaghetti is tender, about 30 minutes. (A small amount of water can be added if necessary.) Sprinkle with cheese. Cover and heat until cheese is melted.

TO COOK IN OVEN: Pour mixture into ungreased 2- or 2½-quart casserole. Cover and bake in 375° oven, stirring occasionally, until spaghetti is tender, about 45 minutes. Uncover; sprinkle with shredded Cheddar cheese and bake about 5 minutes.

## Chili with Macaroni

1 pound ground beef
2 medium onions, chopped (about 1 cup)
1 large green bell pepper, chopped
(about 1 cup)
1 can (28 ounces) whole tomatoes,
undrained
1 can (15 ounces) kidney beans,
undrained
1 can (8 ounces) tomato sauce
1 cup uncooked elbow macaroni (about 3
ounces)
2 to 4 teaspoons chili powder
1 teaspoon salt
1/8 teaspoon ground red pepper (cayenne)
1/8 teaspoon paprika

Cook ground beef, onions and bell pepper in 10-inch skillet, stirring frequently, until beef is brown; drain. Stir in remaining ingredients; break up tomatoes. Heat to boiling; reduce heat. Cover and simmer 20 to 30 minutes, stirring occasionally, until macaroni is tender. **6 servings**

PER SERVING: Calories 360; Protein 24 g; Carbohydrate 35 g; Fat 15 g; Cholesterol 65 mg; Sodium 1090 mg

## Cincinnati-style Chili

*A treat for chili lovers!*

1 pound ground beef
3 medium onions, chopped (about 1 1/2
cups)
1 tablespoon chili powder
1 teaspoon salt
1 can (16 ounces) whole tomatoes,
undrained
1 can (15 1/2 ounces) kidney beans,
undrained
1 can (8 ounces) tomato sauce
1 package (6 or 7 ounces) uncooked
spaghetti
1 1/4 cups shredded Cheddar cheese (5
ounces)

Cook and stir ground beef and about 1 cup of the onions in 3-quart saucepan until beef is brown and onions are tender; drain. Stir in chili powder, salt, tomatoes, beans and tomato sauce; break up tomatoes. Cook uncovered over medium heat until of desired consistency, about 10 minutes.

Cook spaghetti as directed on package; drain. For each serving, spoon about 3/4 cup beef mixture over 1 cup hot spaghetti. Sprinkle each serving with 1/4 cup cheese and about 2 tablespoons remaining onion.

Top with sour cream and sliced hot chili if desired. **5 servings**

PER SERVING: Calories 610; Protein 38 g; Carbohydrate 61 g; Fat 24 g; Cholesterol 80 mg; Sodium 1300 mg

**Cincinnati-style Chili**

## Mostaccioli with Beef and Prosciutto Sauce

*Prosciutto is a type of Italian cured ham, usually sold very thinly sliced.*

1 pound ground beef
2 medium onions, sliced
2 cloves garlic, finely chopped
¾ cup dry red wine or beef broth
2 teaspoons chopped fresh or ½ teaspoon dried rosemary leaves, crushed
1 teaspoon sugar
¼ teaspoon ground nutmeg
¼ teaspoon pepper
1 can (28 ounces) whole tomatoes, undrained
¼ pound prosciutto or dried beef, cut into thin strips
1 pound uncooked mostaccioli or ziti
Grated Parmesan cheese

Cook and stir ground beef, onions and garlic in 10-inch skillet until beef is brown; drain. Stir in remaining ingredients except mostaccioli and cheese; break up tomatoes. Cover and simmer 15 minutes, stirring occasionally.

Uncover and simmer about 1 hour longer, stirring occasionally. Prepare mostaccioli as directed on package; drain. Serve beef mixture over mostaccioli; sprinkle with cheese.

**8 servings**

PER SERVING: Calories 390; Protein 23 g; Carbohydrate 45 g; Fat 13 g; Cholesterol 90 mg; Sodium 480 mg

## Beef and Artichoke Fettuccine

8 ounces uncooked fettuccine
1 jar (6 ounces) marinated artichoke hearts, cut into halves and marinade reserved
1 small onion, finely chopped (about ¼ cup)
1 cup half-and-half
½ cup grated Parmesan cheese
2 cups julienne strips cooked roast beef (about 8 ounces)
Freshly ground pepper
⅓ cup chopped toasted pecans

Cook fettuccine as directed on package. While fettuccine is cooking, heat reserved artichoke marinade in 10-inch skillet over medium heat. Cook onion in marinade about 4 minutes, stirring occasionally. Stir in half-and-half; heat until hot. Stir in Parmesan cheese, artichoke hearts and beef. Heat until hot.

Drain fettuccine; stir into sauce and toss with 2 forks. Sprinkle with pepper and pecans.

**6 servings**

PER SERVING: Calories 320; Protein 20 g; Carbohydrate 28 g; Fat 14 g; Cholesterol 55 mg; Sodium 190 mg

## Beef Goulash

*Goulash originated in Hungary, and this version highlights easy preparation, along with wonderful flavor.*

1½ **pounds ground beef**
1 **medium onion, chopped (about ½ cup)**
1 **stalk celery, sliced**
1 **can (16 ounces) stewed tomatoes**
1 **tomato can water**
1 **package (7 ounces) uncooked elbow**
   **macaroni (2 cups)**
1 **can (6 ounces) tomato paste**
1 **tablespoon Worcestershire sauce**
1 **teaspoon salt**
½ **teaspoon pepper**

Heat oven to 350°. Cook and stir ground beef, onion and celery in 4-quart ovenproof Dutch oven until beef is brown; drain. Stir in remaining ingredients.

Cover and bake until liquid is absorbed and goulash is hot, about 40 minutes; stir.

**6 servings**

PER SERVING: Calories 450; Protein 28 g; Carbohydrate 42 g; Fat 19 g; Cholesterol 65 mg; Sodium 850 mg

MICROWAVE DIRECTIONS: Crumble ground beef into 3-quart microwavable casserole. Cover with waxed paper and microwave on high 4 minutes; stir. Cover with waxed paper and microwave until very little pink remains, 4 to 5 minutes longer; drain.

Substitute 1½ cups hot water for the 1 tomato can water; stir tomatoes, water and remaining ingredients into beef. Cover tightly and microwave until bubbly around edge, about 10 minutes; stir. Cover tightly and microwave, stirring every 5 minutes, until macaroni is tender and liquid is absorbed, 10 to 15 minutes longer.

ITALIAN SAUSAGE GOULASH: Substitute 1½ pounds bulk Italian sausage for the ground beef. Omit salt and pepper.

## Parmesan and Romano Cheese

Romano cheese is made from sheep's milk, not cow's milk, as is Parmesan. Romano has a drier, sharper flavor than Parmesan, and is well suited for pastas served with cured meats such as prosciutto or bacon. Both Romano and Parmesan cheeses add wonderful flavor to pasta, and are at their very best when freshly grated.

*Veal with Spinach and Fettuccine*

## Veal with Spinach and Fettuccine

¾ **pound thin slices lean veal round steak or veal for scallopini**
1 **cup sliced fresh mushrooms (about 3 ounces)**
¼ **cup chopped shallots**
½ **cup Madeira wine or beef broth**
½ **cup beef broth**
2 **teaspoons cornstarch**
⅛ **teaspoon pepper**
1 **package (10 ounces) frozen chopped spinach, thawed and well drained**
2 **cups hot cooked fettuccine**

Cut veal crosswise into ¼-inch strips. Spray 10-inch nonstick skillet with nonstick cooking spray. Sauté veal, mushrooms and shallots in skillet over medium-high heat 3 to 5 minutes or until veal is done. Mix wine, broth, cornstarch and pepper. Stir wine mixture and spinach into skillet. Heat to boiling, stirring constantly. Boil and stir 1 minute. Serve over fettuccine.

**4 servings**

MICROWAVE DIRECTIONS: Decrease wine to ⅓ cup. Trim fat from veal. Cut veal crosswise into ¼-inch strips. Place veal, mushrooms and shallots in 2-quart microwavable casserole. Cover and microwave on high 5 to 6 minutes, stirring every 2 minutes, until veal is done; drain. Mix wine, broth, cornstarch and pepper. Stir wine mixture and spinach into casserole. Cover and microwave 4 to 5 minutes, stirring every 2 minutes, until thickened.

PER SERVING: Calories 255; Protein 20 g; Carbohydrate 23 g; Fat 7 g; Cholesterol 55 mg; Sodium 190 mg

## Minty Lamb Stir-fry

6 **ounces uncooked angel hair pasta**
½ **cup mashed pared kiwifruit (about 2 medium)**
1 **tablespoon chopped fresh or 1 teaspoon dried mint leaves, crushed**
1 **teaspoon cornstarch**
¼ **teaspoon salt**
1 **tablespoon vegetable oil**
¾ **pound lean lamb boneless shoulder or leg, cut into 2 × ¼-inch strips**
1 **clove garlic, finely chopped**
1 **cup julienne strips carrots (about 2 medium)**
1 **cup julienne strips zucchini (about 5 ounces)**

Cook pasta as directed on package; drain. Mix kiwifruit, mint, cornstarch and salt.

Heat oil in 10-inch nonstick skillet over medium-high heat. Stir-fry lamb and garlic about 3 minutes or until lamb is no longer pink. Add carrots and zucchini; stir-fry 2 minutes. Add kiwifruit mixture; stir-fry 1 minute. Serve over pasta.

**4 servings**

PER SERVING: Calories 320; Protein 27 g; Carbohydrate 36 g; Fat 8 g; Cholesterol 105 mg; Sodium 210 mg

## Ground Lamb Stroganoff

*If you like, substitute 1 pound of ground beef for the lamb.*

**1 pound ground lamb**
**1 medium onion, chopped (about ½ cup)**
**1 can (10¾ ounces) condensed cream of chicken soup**
**1 can (4 ounces) mushroom stems and pieces, drained**
**½ teaspoon seasoned salt**
**¼ teaspoon pepper**
**½ cup sour cream or plain yogurt**
**Hot buttered spinach noodles**
**1 medium carrot, finely shredded**

Cook and stir ground lamb and onion in 10-inch skillet until lamb is brown; drain. Stir in soup, mushrooms, seasoned salt and pepper. Heat to boiling; reduce heat. Simmer uncovered, stirring frequently, 5 minutes.

Stir in sour cream; heat just until hot. Serve over noodles; sprinkle with carrot.          **4 servings**

PER SERVING: Calories 595; Protein 28 g; Carbohydrate 49 g; Fat 32 g; Cholesterol 155 mg; Sodium 1000 mg

MICROWAVE DIRECTIONS: Crumble ground lamb into 2-quart microwavable casserole; add onion. Cover with waxed paper and microwave on high 3 minutes; stir. Cover with waxed paper and microwave until no longer pink, 2 to 3 minutes longer; drain.

Stir in soup, mushrooms, seasoned salt and pepper. Cover tightly and microwave 3 minutes; stir. Cover tightly and microwave to boiling, 2 to 3 minutes longer. Stir in sour cream. Cover tightly and microwave until hot, 1 to 2 minutes. Serve over noodles; sprinkle with carrot.

## Frank and Macaroni Casserole

**1 cup uncooked macaroni rings (about 3 ounces)**
**½ cup small curd creamed cottage cheese**
**1 egg, slightly beaten**
**½ teaspoon salt**
**Dash of pepper**
**½ cup shredded sharp Cheddar cheese (2 ounces)**
**2 frankfurters, thinly sliced**
**2 medium tomatoes, sliced**
**1 egg**
**2 tablespoons grated Parmesan cheese**
**⅛ teaspoon dried oregano leaves**

Heat oven to 350°. Grease pie plate, 9 × 1¼ inches. Cook macaroni as directed on package; drain. Mix macaroni, cottage cheese, beaten egg, salt, pepper, Cheddar cheese and frankfurters. Pour into pie plate. Arrange tomatoes on top. Mix egg, Parmesan cheese and oregano; pour over tomatoes. Bake uncovered 25 to 30 minutes or until bubbly.          **5 servings**

PER SERVING: Calories 250; Protein 14 g; Carbohydrate 18 g; Fat 14 g; Cholesterol 130 mg; Sodium 610 mg

## Pork and Pasta Stir-fry

*Great for leftover pasta! If you use cold pasta, it will take a bit longer to heat when added to the stir-fry.*

1¼ pounds lean pork boneless loin or leg
1 teaspoon cornstarch
1 teaspoon soy sauce
¼ teaspoon salt
⅛ teaspoon pepper
2 tablespoons vegetable oil
2 large cloves garlic, finely chopped
¼ to ½ teaspoon crushed red pepper
1 cup ¼-inch diagonal slices celery (about 2 medium stalks)
1 small green or red bell pepper, cut into 1-inch pieces
2 cups bean sprouts (about 4 ounces)
1½ cups sliced mushrooms (about 4 ounces)
2 cups cooked vermicelli
¼ cup sliced green onions with tops (about 3 medium)
1 tablespoon soy sauce

Trim fat from pork loin; cut pork with grain into 2-inch strips. Cut strips across grain into ⅛-inch slices. (For ease in cutting, partially freeze pork, about 1½ hours.) Toss pork, cornstarch, 1 teaspoon soy sauce, the salt and pepper. Cover and refrigerate 20 minutes.

Heat oil in 12-inch nonstick skillet or wok over high heat. Add pork, garlic and red pepper; stir-fry about 5 minutes or until pork is no longer pink. Add celery and bell pepper; stir-fry 2 minutes. Add bean sprouts and mushrooms; stir-fry 2 minutes. Add remaining ingredients; toss about 2 minutes or until thoroughly mixed and hot.                    **6 servings**

PER SERVING: Calories 315; Protein 20 g; Carbohydrate 18 g; Fat 18g; Cholesterol 75 mg; Sodium 460 mg

## Coal Miner's Spaghetti

*This quick, tasty dish is called* Spaghetti alla Carbonara *in Italian.*

1 package (16 ounces) spaghetti
1 clove garlic, finely chopped
1 pound sliced lean bacon, cut into 1-inch pieces
1 tablespoon olive oil
3 eggs
¼ cup grated Parmesan cheese
¼ cup grated Romano cheese
2 tablespoons chopped fresh parsley
½ teaspoon pepper
Grated Parmesan cheese
Freshly ground pepper

Cook spaghetti as directed. Meanwhile cook and stir garlic and bacon in oil until bacon is crisp; drain. Mix eggs, ¼ cup Parmesan cheese, the Romano cheese, parsley and ½ teaspoon pepper; reserve.

Drain spaghetti and immediately return to kettle over very low heat. Toss spaghetti quickly with egg mixture. Add bacon and olive oil mixture and stir. Top with Parmesan cheese; serve with pepper.                    **6 servings**

PER SERVING: Calories 525; Protein 24 g; Carbohydrate 62 g; Fat 20 g; Cholesterol 130 mg; Sodium 560 mg

# Burger Beef Soup

1 pound ground beef
1 small onion, chopped (about ¼ cup)
2 cups tomato juice
1¼ cups water
1 can (10¾ ounces) condensed cream of celery soup
¾ teaspoon chopped fresh or ¼ teaspoon dried basil leaves
¾ teaspoon chopped fresh or ¼ teaspoon dried marjoram leaves
⅛ teaspoon pepper
1 bay leaf
½ cup frozen peas
2 ounces uncooked egg noodles (1 cup)

Cook ground beef and onion in 4-quart Dutch oven over medium heat about 10 minutes, stirring frequently, or until beef is brown; drain. Stir in remaining ingredients except noodles. Heat to boiling. Stir in noodles; reduce heat. Simmer uncovered about 10 minutes, stirring occasionally, until noodles are tender. Remove bay leaf. **4 servings**

PER SERVING: Calories 370; Protein 25 g; Carbohydrate 23 g; Fat 20 g; Cholesterol 85 mg; Sodium 1080 mg

# Tortellini and Sausage Soup

1 pound bulk Italian sausage
1 medium onion, coarsely chopped (about ½ cup)
3 cups water
½ teaspoon dried basil leaves
½ teaspoon dried oregano leaves
2 carrots, sliced
1 medium zucchini or yellow summer squash, halved and sliced
2 cans (10¾ ounces each) condensed tomato soup
8 ounces uncooked dried or frozen cheese- or meat-filled tortellini (2 cups)
Grated Parmesan cheese

Cook and stir sausage and onion in 4-quart Dutch oven until sausage is light brown; drain. Stir in remaining ingredients except cheese.

Heat to boiling; reduce heat. Cover and simmer until vegetables and tortellini are tender, about 20 minutes. Serve with cheese. **6 servings**

PER SERVING: Calories 445; Protein 24 g; Carbohydrate 29 g; Fat 26 g; Cholesterol 115 mg; Sodium 1570 mg

**Tortellini and Sausage Soup**

# METRIC CONVERSION GUIDE

| U.S. UNITS | CANADIAN METRIC | AUSTRALIAN METRIC |
|---|---|---|
| **Volume** | | |
| 1/4 teaspoon | 1 mL | 1 ml |
| 1/2 teaspoon | 2 mL | 2 ml |
| 1 teaspoon | 5 mL | 5 ml |
| 1 tablespoon | 15 mL | 20 ml |
| 1/4 cup | 50 mL | 60 ml |
| 1/3 cup | 75 mL | 80 ml |
| 1/2 cup | 125 mL | 125 ml |
| 2/3 cup | 150 mL | 170 ml |
| 3/4 cup | 175 mL | 190 ml |
| 1 cup | 250 mL | 250 ml |
| 1 quart | 1 liter | 1 liter |
| 1 1/2 quarts | 1.5 liter | 1.5 liter |
| 2 quarts | 2 liters | 2 liters |
| 2 1/2 quarts | 2.5 liters | 2.5 liters |
| 3 quarts | 3 liters | 3 liters |
| 4 quarts | 4 liters | 4 liters |
| **Weight** | | |
| 1 ounce | 30 grams | 30 grams |
| 2 ounces | 55 grams | 60 grams |
| 3 ounces | 85 grams | 90 grams |
| 4 ounces (1/4 pound) | 115 grams | 125 grams |
| 8 ounces (1/2 pound) | 225 grams | 225 grams |
| 16 ounces (1 pound) | 455 grams | 500 grams |
| 1 pound | 455 grams | 1/2 kilogram |

| Measurements | | Temperatures | |
|---|---|---|---|
| Inches | Centimeters | Fahrenheit | Celsius |
| 1 | 2.5 | 32° | 0° |
| 2 | 5.0 | 212° | 100° |
| 3 | 7.5 | 250° | 120° |
| 4 | 10.0 | 275° | 140° |
| 5 | 12.5 | 300° | 150° |
| 6 | 15.0 | 325° | 160° |
| 7 | 17.5 | 350° | 180° |
| 8 | 20.5 | 375° | 190° |
| 9 | 23.0 | 400° | 200° |
| 10 | 25.5 | 425° | 220° |
| 11 | 28.0 | 450° | 230° |
| 12 | 30.5 | 475° | 240° |
| 13 | 33.0 | 500° | 260° |
| 14 | 35.5 | | |
| 15 | 38.0 | | |

**NOTE**

The recipes in this cookbook have not been developed or tested using metric measures. When converting recipes to metric, some variations in quality may be noted.

# Index

About Pasta
  Amounts, 47
  Cooking Timetable (chart), *vii*
  Dried and Fresh, 52
  Flavored, Water, 33
  Flour for, 3
  Identification Guide, *viii–ix*
  Low-Calorie, 18
  Menus, *xi*
  Parmesan and Romano
    Cheese, 73
  Perk Up, 21
  Sauces, 13
  Tomatoes, 61
  Varying Pasta, 44
  Yields, *vi*
Amatricina Sauce, 11
Angel Hair Pasta
  in Garlic Sauce, 21
  Lamb Stir-fry, Minty, 75
  with Shrimp, 50
Antonio's Fettuccine Alfredo, 7
Artichoke Fettuccine, Beef and,
  72

Baked Macaroni with Beef and
  Cheese, 64
Baked Spaghetti Sauce, 10
Baja Chicken-Pasta Salad, 44
Balsamic Vinaigrette, 28
Bean(s), Chili, and Pasta, 30
Beef
  Casserole, Easy, 65
  Fettuccine, and Artichoke, 72
  Goulash, 73
  Lasagne, 62
    Quick, 61
    Roll-ups, 62
    with Two Sauces, Green,
      63
  Macaroni with, Cheese,
    Baked, 64
  Manicotti, 64
  Meatballs
    in Dijon Sauce, 67
    and Noodles, Sauerbraten,
      69
    Spaghetti and, 66–67
    in Tomato Sauce, 10
  and Noodles, Skillet, 65
  Sauce
    and Proscuitto, Mostaccioli
      with, 72
    Baked Spaghetti, 10
    Bolognese, 11
    in Red Wine, Ground, 66
    Tomato, Pasta with
      Chunky, 65
  Soup, Burger, 78
  Spaghetti, One-Skillet, 69
Bolognese Sauce, 11
Bolognese Sauce, Ravioli with, 8

Bow-ties
  with Cilantro Pesto, 43
  Salad, Tarragon-Seafood, 58
  Tuna Toss, 55
Broccoli
  Chicken-Pasta, Primavera, 36
  Chicken Pasta, Tarragon
    and, 33
  Noodles with, and Ricotta
    Sauce, Half-Shell, 1
  Shells with Chicken and, 36
Burger Beef Soup, 78

Cajun Seafood and Noodles,
  47
Capellini. *See.* Angel Hair
  Pasta
Cheese(y)
  About Parmesan and Ro-
    mano, 73
  Casserole, Tuna-Asparagus,
    53
  Chile con Queso, 25
  Chili Beans and Pasta, 30
  Cottage Filling, 63
  Lasagne, 62
    Cheesy, 27
    Quick, 61
    Roll-ups, 62
    with Two Sauces, Green,
      63
    Seafood, 54
    Vegetable, 26
  Macaroni
    and, 24
    with Beef and, Baked, 64
    Casserole, Frank and, 76
    and, with Green Chilies, 24
    con Queso, 25
    Salad, -Shrimp, 57
    Salmon and, 54
  Manicotti, 28, 64
  Noodles with Broccoli and, Ri-
    cotta Sauce, Half-Shell,
    1
  Noodles Romanoff, 27
  Ravoli, Pumpkin, 8
  Ravioli with Bolognese
    Sauce, 7
  Salad, Macaroni-Shrimp, 57
  Salmon and Macaroni, 54
  Shells, Seafood-stuffed, 55
  Spaghetti, Coal Miner's, 77
  Spaghetti, One-Skillet, 68
  Tortelli with Olive Sauce, 5
  Tortellini, Three-, 25
Chicken
  and Broth, 41
  with Cellophane Noodles,
    Thia, 35
  Farfalle with Cilantro Pesto,
    43

Lasagne with Two Sauces,
  Green, 63
Linguine with, and Artichoke
  Hearts, 35
Noodles, -Basil, 34
Penne with Vodka Sauce, 34
Primavera, 36
Salad
  Baja, -Pasta, 44
  -Pasta, 43
  -Cucumber, 43
  Macaroni, -Cantaloupe, 44
  Italian, 44
Shells with, and Broccoli, 36
Soup, Noodle, 40
Taragon and, 33
Tetrazzini, 39
Chili con Queso, 25
Chili Beans and Pasta, 30
Clam Sauce, Red, 15
Clam Sauce, White, 15
Coal Miner's Spaghetti, 77
Cooking Time Table (Chart), *vii*
Curried Turkey Spaghetti, 39

Dilled Pasta Salad with
  Smoked Fish, 57

Easy Beef Casserole, 65
Egg Noodles, 2

Farfalle
  with Cilantro Pesto, 43
  Salad, Tarragon-Seafood, 58
  Tuna Toss, 55
Fettuccini
  Antonio's, Alfredo, 7
  Beef and Artichoke, 72
  Beef in Red Wine Sauce,
    Ground, 66
  Scallops, Spicy, 48
  Scampi with, 49
  Veal with Spinach and, 75
Flavored Pasta Water, 38
Flour for Pasta, 3
Frank and Macaroni Casserole,
  76
Fusilli, Savory, 17

Garlic Sauce, Angel Hair Pasta
  in, 21
Ginger Dressing, 58
Goulash, Beef, 73
Green Lasagne with Two
  Sauces, 63
Ground Beef in Red Wine
  Sauce, 66–67
Ground Lamb Stroganoff, 76

Half-Shell Noodles with Broccoli and Ricotta Sauce, 1
Ham Tetrazzini, and Turkey, 40

Herbs
  Chicken, and Tarragon, 33
  Chicken-Basil, Noodles, 34
  Lamb Stir-fry, Minty, 75
  Pesto, 13
  Salad
    Macaroni, Pesto-, 31
    Pasta, with Smoked Fish,
      Dilled, 57
    Seafood, -Tarragon, 58
  Vermicelli with Fresh, 18

Italian Pasta Salad, 44

Lamb Stir-fry, Minty, 75
Lamb Stroganoff, Ground, 76
  Lasagne, 62
  Cheesy, 27
  Quick, 61
  Roll-ups, 62
  Seafood, 54
  with Two Sauces, Green, 62
  Vegetable, 26
Linguine with Chicken and Arti-
  choke Hearts, 35
Low-Calorie Pasta, 18

Macaroni. *See also* Shells
  with Beef and Cheese,
    Baked, 64
  Casserole, Easy Beef, 65
  Casserole, Frank and, 76
  and Cheese, 24
  and Cheese with Green Chil-
    ies, 24
  Chili Beans and Pasta, 30
  Goulash, Beef, 73
  con Queso
    Salad, Chicken-Cantaloupe,
      44
    Chicken-Cucumber, 43
    Pesto-, 31
    -Shrimp, 57
    Tomato-Pasta, 31
  Salmon and, 54
  Tuna-, Skillet, 52
Manicotti, 28, 64
Meatballs
  in Dijon Sauce, 67
  and Noodles, Sauerbraten,
    69
  Spaghetti and, 66–67
  in Tomato Sauce, 10
Minty Lamb Stir-fry, 75
Mostaccioli with Beef and Pro-
  sciutto Sauce, 72
Mostaccioli with Bell Pepper
  and Basil, 17
Mushroom(s)
  Sauce, and Brandy, 13
  Tarragon and Chicken, 33
  Tuna Noodles Romanoff, 53

Soup, Turkey Tortellini, 41
Veal with Spinach and Fettuc-
ine, 75

Noodle(s)
Beef and, Skillet, 65
with Broccoli and Ricotta
Sauce, Half-Shell, 1
Casserole, Tuna-Asparagus,
53
Cellophane, Thai Chicken
with, 35
Chicken-Basil, 34
Egg, 2
Lamb Stroganoff, Ground, 76
Lasagne, 62
Cheesy, 27
Quick, 61
Roll-ups, 62
Seafood, 54
with Two Sauces, Green,
63
Vegetable, 26
Meatballs in Dijon Sauce, 67
Meatballs and, Sauerbraten,
69
Romanoff, Tuna, 53
Scallops in Cream Sauce, 49
Seafood and, Cajun, 47
Soup, Burger Beef, 78
Soup, Chicken, 40
Spinach, 6

Olive(s)
Fusilli, Savory, 17
Penne with Vodka Sauce, 34
Salad with Smoked Fish,
Dilled, 57
Sauce, Tortelli with, 5
Tetrazzini, Turkey and Ham,
40
One-Skillet Spaghetti, 69
Orzo Salad, Baja Chicken-, 44

Pasta with Chunky Tomato
Sauce, 65
Pasta Shells with Chicken and
Broccoli, 36
Penne with Radicchio, 22
Penne with Vodka Sauce, 34
Perk Up Pasta, 21
Pesto, 13
Cilantro, Farfalle with, 43
Salad, -Macaroni, 31
Pork and Pasta Stir-fry, 77
Pumpkin Ravioli, 9
Pumpkin Sauce, Seed, 8

Quick Lasagne, 61

Radicchio, Penne with, 22
Ravioli with Bolognese Sauce, 8
Red Clam Sauce, 15

Romanoff, Noodles, 27
Seafood Pasta with Vegetables, 48

Salad
Chicken, 43
Baja, 44
-Cucumber, 43
Italian, 44
-Macaroni, -Cantaloupe, 44
Dressing, Ginger, 58
Macaroni, Pesto, 31
Pasta with Smoked Fish,
Dilled, 57
Tomato-Pasta, 31
Turkey-Pasta, with Spinach
Sauce, 45
Salmon and Macaroni, 54
Sauce(s)
About, 13
Amatriciana, 11
Asparagus, Ziti with, 22
Beef and Proscuitto, Mostacci-
oli with, 72
Bolognese, 11
Bolognese, Ravioli with, 7
Broccoli and Ricotta, Half-
Shell Noodles with, 1
Clam, Red, 15
Clam, White, 15
Creamy, 63
Dijon, Meatballs in, 67
Garlic, Angel Hair Pasta in,
21
Lasagne with Two, Green, 63
Meat, 63
Mushroom and Brandy, 13
Mussel, Spaghetti with, 52
Olive, Tortelli with, 5
Pesto, 13
Pesto, Farfalle with Cilantro,
43
Pumpkin Seed, 9
Red Wine, Ground Beef in,
66
Spaghetti, Baked, 10
Spinach, Turkey-Pasta, Salad
with, 45
Sugo, 11
Tomato, Meatballs in, 10
Tomato, Pasta with Chunky,
65
Vodka, Penne with, 34
White, 26
Sausage
Bolognese Sauce, 11
Meat Sauce, 63
Soup, Tortellini and, 78
Sauerbraten Meatballs and Noo-
dles, 68
Savory Fusilli, 17
Scallops in Cream Sauce, 49
Scampi with Fettuccine, 49

Seafood
Lasagne, 54
Lobster, Shell macaroni with,
50
Mussel Sauce, Spaghetti
with, 52
and Noodles, Cajun, 47
Salad (Pasta), 58
Macaroni-Shrimp, 57
Tarragon-, 58
Scallops, Spicy, 48
Scallops in Cream Sauce, 49
Scampi with Fettuccine, 49
Shells, -stuffed, 55
Shrimp, Angel Hair Pasta
with, 50
with Vegetables, 48
Shell(s) Macaroni
Chicken-, Primavera, 36
with Chicken and Broccoli,
36
with Lobster, 50
Salad, Tomato-Pasta, 31
Seafood-stuffed, 55
Skillet Beef and Noodles, 65
Smoked Fish, Dilled Pasta
Salad with, 57
Soup
Burger Beef, 78
Chicken and Broth, 41
Chicken Noodle, 40
Tortellini, 30
Tortellini and Sausage, 78
Turkey Tortellini, 41
Spaghetti
Coal Miner's, 77
and Meatballs, 66–67
with Mussel Sauce, 52
One-Skillet, 69
Sauce, Baked, 10
Tetrazzini, Chicken, 39
Terrazzini, Turkey and Ham,
40
Turkey, Curried, 39
Spicy Scallops, 48
Spinach
and Chicken, Tarragon, 33
Lasagne Roll-ups, 62
Manicotti, 28
Noodles, 6
Ravioli with Bolognese
Sauce, 7
Salad, Pesto-Macaroni, 31
Salad with Spinach Sauce,
Turkey, 45
Tortelli with Olive Sauce, 5
Veal with, and Fettuccine, 75
Vermicelli with, 18
Spiral Macaroni
Tarragon and Chicken Pasta,
33
Salad
Chicken, 43

Italian, 44
Turkey Pasta, with Spinach
Sauce, 45
Straw and Hay Pasta, 7
Sugo Sauce, 11

Tarragon and Chicken Pasta,
33
Tarragon-Seafood Salad, 58
Thai Chicken with Cellophane
Noodles, 35
Three-Cheese Tortellini, 25
Tomato(es)
About, 61
Salad, -Pasta, 31
Sauce, Meatballs in, 10
Sauce, Pasta with Chunky,
65
Tortelli with Olive Sauce, 5
Tortellini
in Balsamic Vinaigrette, 28
Soup, 30
Soup, and Sausage, 78
Soup, Turkey, 41
Three-Cheese, 25
Tuna
Casserole, -Asparagus, 53
-Macaroni Skillet, 52
Noodles Romanoff, 53
Toss, 55
Turkey
with Pesto, 38
Primavera, 38
Salad with Spinach Sauce,
-Pasta, 45
Soup, Tortellini, 41
Spaghetti, Curried, 39
Tetrazzini, and Ham, 40

Varying Pasta, 44
Veal with Spinach and Fettuc-
cine, 75
Vegetable(s)
Bell Pepper and Basil, Mos-
taccioli with, 17
Lasagne, 26
Seafood Pasta, with, 48
Vermicelli with Lemony
Green, 21
Vermicelli
with Fresh Herbs, 18
with Lemony Green Vegeta-
bles, 21
Salad, Seafood-Pasta, 58
and Spinach, 18
Stir-fry, Pork and Pasta,
77
Vinaigrette, Balsamic, 28

White Sauce, 26
White Clam Sauce, 15

Ziti with Asparagus Sauce,
22